Corporate Management and Financial Planning

Corporate Management and Financial Planning

The British Rail Experience

John Harris and Glyn Williams

PAUL ELEK
GRANADA PUBLISHING
London Toronto Sydney New York

Published by Granada Publishing in Paul Elek Ltd 1980

Granada Publishing Limited
Frogmore, St Albans, Herts AL2 2NF
and
3 Upper James Street, London W1R 4BP
Suite 405, 4th Floor, 866 United Nations Plaza, New York, NY 10017, USA
117 York Street, Sydney, NSW 2000, Australia
100 Skyway Avenue, Rexdale, Ontario M9W 3A6, Canada
PO Box 84165, Greenside, 2034 Johannesburg, South Africa
61 Beach Road, Auckland, New Zealand

British Library Cataloguing in Publication Data
Harris, John
Corporate management and financial planning.
1. British Rail – Finance
2. Corporations – Finance – Case studies
3. Corporate planning – Case studies
I. Title II. Williams, Glyn.
658.1'51   HE2231

ISBN 0-246-11435-5

Phototypesetting by Parkway Group, London and Abingdon
Printed in Great Britain by Richard Clay (The Chaucer Press) Ltd., Bungay, Suffolk

Granada ®
Granada Publishing ®

Contents

Preface

This book is concerned with developing a theory of financial planning within the broader subject of corporate planning theory and testing this theory against the experience of one organisation, British Rail. British Rail was chosen partly because of the background and experience of the authors, but also because it has been a leader in the development and application of the ideas of financial planning.

Chapter 2 describes and discusses, in theoretical terms, the concepts of financial planning when undertaken within a corporate planning framework. This is not the only book that links corporate and financial planning, but we have aimed to link them in a more rigorous manner than hitherto and in a manner more suitable to both theoretical and practical considerations. Chapter 3 also deals with the theoretical links; it emphasises the structures, processes and techniques necessary for sound financial planning within a corporate planning framework. Subsequent chapters examine the links from a practical point of view using the experience of British Rail as exemplary material and B.R. data as source information for most tables and figures.

We believe that, because of this approach, the book will appeal to a number of audiences. In the first place it will appeal to students of many disciplines who wish to be informed about the theory, problems and opportunities associated with financial planning when linked closely with corporate planning. Secondly, the book contains a great deal of information about British Rail. The railway 'buff' will therefore find it interesting and useful in updating his knowledge of fundamental issues in transport policy. But because British Rail's experience is used as a case study, financial planners in other organisations, in both private and public sectors, may be interested in considering whether the theoretical framework is comprehensive enough for them to use. In particular, they may be interested in evaluating the success of the links we suggest, as far as they have been applied in British Rail, and making comparisons with their own organisations.

In developing the ideas associated with the book, we have been helped by a number of people, who have commented on earlier drafts and/or provided us with information. In particular, we would wish to acknowledge publicly the great help that we received from British Rail. It is always invidious to thank only certain individuals in circumstances in which so many helped. It would be remiss, however, not to thank Derek Fowler, Fred Sykes and Peter Linney of British Rail individually for their contributions. We are also grateful to Professor C. T. Tomkins, Mr G. H. Ray and Mr B. C. L. Davies of the University of Bath for their useful comments.

In addition we would like to thank David Jones, formerly Executive Director, Finance and Financial Controller of British Rail, who was to have been a co-author of this book until the pressures of his assuming a new post made this impossible. Up to that time, David made a considerable contribution to the development of our ideas through lively and challenging discussions. Moreover he greatly encouraged our efforts by pointing us towards the 'right people to see'.

Finally, we would like to acknowledge the help and encouragement of those who typed various parts of drafts, or complete drafts, of the book, viz Julie and Glenys our respective wives. Glenys, in particular, should be thanked because she produced not only many 'drafts' but also a beautiful new daughter called Jenny, in between chapters.

DJH
DGW
December, 1979

ONE

Introduction

Most people would recognise that the planning of an organisation's finances is of paramount importance to its survival and success. This has been and still is, in essence, the prime concern of financial planning. However, the methods used to achieve these ends have changed as the subject has developed over the 1970s. Much of the available evidence shows, for example, that financial planning has become more formalised with the increasing use of computers. It is also clear that financial planning has become more commonly used in the determination of business activities rather than just working out the financial implications of what has been planned.

This book examines the skills needed by financial planners to cope with their traditional roles and those imposed by the newer developments. However, the approach suggested here goes much further in that it argues for a change of focus in financial planning, emphasising the need for financial planning to take place within a corporate planning framework. Moreover, the book is concerned with examining not only the technical subtleties of financial planning but also the processes and structures needed on a corporate level to ensure that technical competence is transformed into successful management. Thus, the book develops a normative theory for linking financial and corporate planning.

To consider the practical implications of that theory and the linking of financial planning with corporate planning, we have chosen to study the experience of British Rail in this context. British Rail would be a fascinating industry for study in its own right because of the controversy that continually seems to surround it and because of its size and importance in the economic structure of the country. Whilst

1

some of these have been discussed by Pryke and Dodgson,[1] new events have overtaken the picture as seen by them. In particular, a major review of transport policy has been conducted and a consultative document[2] has already been produced together with the British Rail reply[3] and a Government White Paper.[4] These provide interesting and relevant issues, both for the student of financial planning and for those who wish to study the general problems of nationalised industries as exemplified by British Rail. Moreover, British Rail is currently undertaking an extensive review of its strategic options to determine a sense of direction for each of its businesses and their sectors. Additionally, British Rail is likely to be affected by changes being developed in a wider context, particularly with respect to the E.E.C. Regulations and possible changes that nationalised industries may be asked to make as a result of the 1976 N.E.D.O. Report[5] and the related White Paper.[6]

However strong the case may be for treating the subjects separately, in our view it is important both to understand the theoretical points of, and the normative links between, financial planning and corporate planning. It is no less important to consider these points and links in a particular set of circumstances; that is, to consider how financial planning in a corporate framework operates in practice and to suggest improvements that have a chance of succeeding in the real world and are not merely 'pie in the sky' suggestions. Thus, although the main emphasis will be on financial planning issues these will be illustrated with examples from the British Rail experience. Given the background of one of the authors and taking note of the comments made above, it is not surprising that the examples should be taken from the experience of British Rail. In addition the experience of British Rail in financial planning, its involvement in the development of corporate plans, its past uneasy (but now improved) relationship with government and government agencies and the implications of new and evolving major constraints such as 'cash limits' add further variety to the relevant and interesting material to be found in the industry. This should not limit the usefulness of this book to students of the nationalised industries sector, for increasingly issues such as these affect more and more organisations, in both the public and private sectors. Indeed, one of the purposes of this study is to argue that nationalised industries are a part of the total spectrum of organisations attempting to achieve the same kind of objectives as firms in the private sector but are not allowed to do so to the same degree because of constraints imposed on them by government. While the constraints may be highlighted in the case of nationalised industries, organisations in the private sector are subject to the same kind of constraints, particularly with respect to responding to the various requests of government.

Financial planning can provide a means through which these constraints can be identified and eased, if not removed. This will be the case more particularly when the financial planning procedures are fully integrated with or represent the corporate plans; when they are linked with making judgements about the nature of the total business in the future and making the appropriate adjustments so as to ensure that the business actually gets to its objectives. As yet, this does not seem to have been achieved by British Rail but the organisation is heavily involved in these processes and, as we have stated, is subject to as many, if not more, constraints than most other businesses. Furthermore, it will be noted that neither the form of the constraints nor their interpretation over time has remained constant. Indeed, the N.E.D.O. Report pointed out that the relationships between the British Railways Board and the Department of the Environment were such that neither knew what was expected of the other.[7] However, the relationship between government and British Rail has improved significantly subsequent to the N.E.D.O. Report.

1.1 Financial planning

Financial planning is not undertaken in British Rail merely as a defence against uncertainties but rather because of the belief that it provides the organisation with a means of planning and using resources more efficiently in relation to their objectives. An exhaustive consideration of why this should be so is developed and discussed in chapters 2, 3 and 6, but we need to develop further the theme of why it is that we concentrate on financial planning aspects of corporate planning. As was noted earlier, there has been a substantial change in the nature of financial planning over the last decade. The traditional roles required of the financial planner have always touched on such areas as forecasting and pricing as well as general financial management, investment appraisal, budgetary control and costing but not as part of an overall planning process; that is, as part of a corporate plan.

It has also become increasingly the case that financial planners not only evaluate and monitor the plans of others but are also actively involved in the determination of these plans. Part of this derives from the tendency to move away from the concept of a central group of planners who are divorced from the rest of the organisation and substituting, instead, a modular approach to planning in which parts of a plan are 'grown' within specialist departments and integrated by the central planners by committee procedures. Equally, as corporate planning becomes more established as a powerful and complete form of planning, financial planning is also recognised as an integral part of corporate planning which increasingly uses computers to overcome the sheer physical difficulties experienced in the past.

All of these skills are examined in detail in chapters 2 and 3, in terms of describing their nature and in examining how they may be related, theoretically, within a normative framework. In chapter 6 the skills and their relationships, as exemplified by the structure of British Rail, are considered in a practical context. While it is well understood, even in theoretical terms, that the processes of planning are complex and interactive, it is less well understood that the management of such processes is exceedingly difficult. Thus, this chapter will examine the current procedures through which financial planning is undertaken and comment on their effectiveness. It will deal, for example, with the interaction of financial and corporate planning, demonstrating, *inter alia,* that financial planning can no longer be concerned with merely extrapolating past trends with appropriate adjustments for inflation, but must take a more fundamental stance by asking and seeking answers to questions such as where do we want to be in the future and how can we plan to get there? Financial planning on its own may not answer such questions entirely–only corporate planning can do that–but financial planning can and should make an important contribution to answering these questions.

The formulation of such questions is not particularly new. Informally it must have been done throughout time, but formally this has only been done in the last twenty years or so. With the aid of computers, formalisation has gone further so that now there are 'corporate models' which help answer these questions. It seems clear that 'corporate modelling' is beginning to be used extensively. For example Grinyer and Wooller, in their survey of sixty-five companies, found that most of the companies started to develop corporate models after 1970.[8] Although corporate models mean in detail all things to all men, the most widespread use of corporate models was for purposes of financial planning.[9] Five years seemed to be the most popular planning horizon but a ten-year period was also sometimes used. Those models with a one-year planning horizon seemed to be used as budgeting models. Whatever the detail of this survey and no matter whether we argue that corporate planning comes before or after financial planning, the implications of this trend are that financial planners will need to be familiar with concepts of model building, computer technology and the determination of corporate objectives as well as the means through which they are to be achieved. In this book greatest emphasis will be put on the relationship of financial planning to the development and implementation of corporate plans.

1.2 British Railways Board

We have already noted that one of our main concerns will be with financial planning in general and theoretical terms and its relationship to corporate planning. A second main concern will be to discuss these generalities within a realistic framework. While it may be reasonably easy to understand the underlying skills necessary for financial planning, the difficulties of managing those skills are less easily understood unless they are put into a framework to which people can relate. Hence, the purpose of chapters 4 and 5 is to provide a framework by providing a description and analysis of the main activities and problems of British Rail.

It may be advisable at this point to emphasise that British Rail is made up of many businesses including not only the railways, but also shipping, catering, hotels, engineering, property and hovercraft. As will be seen in detail later, the British Railways Board controls a very large business, measured by any of the usual criteria, but it is also made up of a set of businesses which are quite fundamentally different one from another. Even within these businesses, activities are undertaken that vary quite considerably one from another. For example, Railways will include freight and parcels, and on the passenger side inter-city services, the major commuter network of London and the South East, other provincial commuter services and other provincial rural services. Each of these business activities demonstrates different characteristics, particularly with respect to such things as use of the service in general, use of the service at certain times–the 'peak' problem–and the market characteristics. Whilst each of the large businesses competes for British Railways funds and resources there is also a problem of fund allocation within each business–for example, freight competing with passenger.

In this respect, British Railways exemplifies many of the planning features and characteristics of large firms in the private sector which arise out of its size, its needs for large amounts of funds, control of large numbers of employees and with a heterogeneous set of objectives. But, of course, British Rail is not a firm in the private sector. It is a nationalised industry and this brings with it constraints and responsibilities that firms in the private sector may not feel, at least as explicitly as in public undertakings. Particularly important in this respect is the relationship of British Rail to government.

In strictly legal terms whilst the industry is not answerable to Parliament for its day-to-day running, it is answerable ultimately to the Secretary of State of the Department of Transport for a number of things which will be examined in detail later. For the purpose of this introduction it is sufficient to indicate that, while it seems to be no longer true, in the past this relationship has been an uneasy one and has sometimes lacked continuity and consistency. In addition there seemed to have been a lack of guidelines as to what was expected of the organisation and the overall framework within which the organisation was expected to operate had become blurred. More recently, complaints referring to the uncertainty that surrounds the intentions of central government have arisen from most of the nationalised industries. This uncertainty has caused the task of investment planning in nationalised industries to be harder than it should have been.

It should not necessarily be thought that, because relationships between government and industry seem to be more direct in the case of nationalised industries, these relationships do not exist for organisations in the private sector. They may not exist explicitly or formally, but what the government does or does not do is an important influence on the well-being of these organisations. This is clear from a consideration of the performance of firms in the private sector and the monetary and fiscal policies adopted by the government of the day. Of course, this is not the only consideration that has to be taken into account. There has been increasing evidence that central government wishes to 'plan' the future with organisations in the private sector as well as with public undertakings. Thus, larger private firms have been asked to draw up such things as 'planning agreements' on a voluntary basis. These may determine a more direct relationship between industry and government which may affect the performance of an organisation. It is not the purpose of this book to argue that such direct relationships should or should not exist. It is part of our remit, however, to examine the relationship of corporate and financial planning to such agreements. Given the experience of British Rail, there is a wealth of knowledge to be gained by examining the relationship between government and one nationalised industry. From this experience, which is covered in chapter 7, it is clear that it is difficult to achieve lasting agreements between the parties. It is also clear that, while it may be desirable to have agreements, there may be dangers if these are not based on the carefully evaluated options considered in a corporate planning framework. The government and other companies may therefore learn much from studying the British Rail experience in developing its financial and corporate planning.

1.3 Issues in financial planning in British Rail

There are a number of issues in British Rail's history that provide useful guidelines to financial planning within a corporate framework. For example, there is the great deal of experience in British Rail of financial planning. In spite of this, however, it is generally agreed that since the early 1950s the railways have experienced successive financial crises. There have been many financial plans taking many forms, but it is claimed–certainly by the government–that these and policy reviews 'all have failed to provide a stable financial framework for this important national asset'.[10]

It is not the intention of this book to regurgitate the conventional reasons to explain why this situation exists such as the growth of road competition and the rapid inflation of recent years. These are undoubtedly important reasons but our main purpose is to consider the role of financial planning in anticipating such changes and to 'proact' rather than to react to such situations. What seems reasonably clear from British Rail's experience is that this task has been made more difficult by changing government requirements, which have often led to financial plans being drawn up as palliatives rather than trying to eradicate the roots of British Rail's fundamental problems.

British Rail has as much experience as any other organisation in the use of corporate and financial planning. What makes the study of its situation interesting is that it has grown and fostered in external conditions which appear hostile, at least on face value. This hostility to planning is not unique to British Rail. As the N.E.D.O. Report pointed out there was a lack of trust and mutual understanding between many of the nationalised industries and those in government concerned with their affairs. Moreover, it pointed out that there was no systematic framework for agreement on long term objectives and strategy and no assurance of continuity when decisions were reached, and this was partly due to the different time-scales used by the industries and government bodies. As far as British Rail is concerned, in the past seventeen years, starting with Beeching, a considerable amount of planning has been conducted. There have been the equivalent of six corporate plans, the first being developed under that name as early as 1970 and that was not all. There have been additional major studies such as Network Studies carried out by the Finance Department, the 1968 Freight Plan, other appraisals undertaken by the Department of the Environment and a series of Interim Rail Strategies each of which was concerned with certain aspects of planning which might now be described as 'corporate'. There is thus a wealth of experience of actually constructing a corporate plan.

All of these have had to be scrapped or only partially implemented, not so much because they were not well done, but because of other factors. These include changes in government policy, problems resulting from rapid inflation or, in the case of the Fourth Corporate Plan, because it did not meet British Rail's broadly perceived objectives. Consequently, it is necessary to consider the need for government to provide the right environment for future planning, whether it be financial or any other kind of planning. If major discontinuities are introduced by government action, this may mean the end of meaningful and purposeful planning, not only in British Rail but organisations in the private sector as well. Instead, industries may lurch from one crisis to another, merely reacting to circumstances as they find them. This could have serious implications as far as company objectives are concerned, for it may well be that, in these circumstances, companies may wish to concentrate on survival by way of having a great deal of flexibility either in terms of having a broad product–market mix or in terms of large amounts of liquid resources. As far as the former is concerned, this may not be possible for nationalised industries, because of the obligations set upon them in their Establishment Acts and in subsequent legislation, particularly in the *1962 Transport Act* in the case of British Rail.

Another theme to be discussed in the study is the effect of organisational structure on the development and success of financial and corporate plans. For example, in the case of British Rail it has been argued that 'One of the most important reasons for the railways' financial collapse has been the lack of any countervailing force within the organisation to offset the understandable pressure which builds up from operating departments for investment in the latest and most modern type of equipment.'[11] It is clearly important to consider the appropriate organisational structure so that the contribution that financial planning can make to the well-being of the organisation is enhanced rather than frustrated.

In addition there are a number of current issues that make the discussion of financial planning in British Rail topical. One of these concerns the relationship of British Rail to the European Economic Community. In practice Britain's membership of the E.E.C. has not yet had a major effect on shaping the domestic transport policy of this country. Nevertheless, there are areas under study that could have a significant effect on transport operations in the United Kingdom if they ever become legislation. Chapter 7 will consider British Rail's financial planning procedures in an E.C.C. context as well as moves towards harmonisation of procedures.

Another issue which is highly topical relates to the imposition of cash limits in the determination of future patterns of grant assistance and investment. This applies not only in transport but for other organisations as well and may in future apply to more. As far as British Rail is concerned, however, it means a major change. Up to 1968 British Rail for many years had been in the position of deficit financing; that is, open-ended subsidisation. It was argued by some[12] that this resulted in demoralisation of staff and was the major reason why the Railways Board has in the past been unable or unwilling to fulfil its predications as to performance or financial viability. The assertion was also made that such an open-ended subsidisation has resulted in a lax attitude being taken towards capital expenditure which Railway management–it was argued by Pryke and Dodgson– had seen necessary for the creation of a perfect railway system regardless of capital required. From 1968 British Rail, theoretically, has not been allowed to practise deficit financing, but, as we shall see in chapter 5, this has caused major problems and led to a further capital reconstruction. We shall also see in chapter 5 that British Rail has been subjected to a number of other financial controls which included being asked to break even on the freight side with the passenger side being allowed a special overall grant called a Public Service Obligation, the extent of which is controlled under a cash limit procedure.

Whatever the reason, it is clear that the change to cash limits may have dramatic and important implications on the shape of the railway of the future. It may have implications for staff morale and outlook on investment procedures. Although, as we shall see in chapter 5, the movement from uncontrolled deficit financing to grant aid cash limits has, in practice, been interrupted by other constraints imposed by financial considerations, the movement has meant that financial planners in British Rail have had to re-think and re-formulate their ideas. The exposure to this process of re-thinking and re-formulation will be of invaluable use to others not so dramatically and fundamentally affected as in British Rail.

Finally, there are more speculative issues. There is, for example, the long-term need for transport policy to be comprehensively reviewed with the consultative documents being the first stage in that process. There is the possibility that government may resurrect the argument that financial planning (and corporate planning) should be undertaken on a more integrated basis; that is, British Rail might have to co-operate more extensively with the other transport operators in the determination of future plans. So, instead of planning for the future largely in isolation, but taking competition into account, it may be that the Department of Transport might attempt to plan the total transport market and then allocate parts of it to road, rail, canals, coastal shipping and airways. Even if we do not accept that the integrated approach will be attempted in the near future, there remain controversial strategic issues in British Rail such as whether British Rail ought to attempt to hive off part of its parcels traffic as well as procedural issues such as the role of Department of Transport officials in the corporate/financial planning process. Most of these issues are considered in chapter 9.

1.4 Summary

Financial planning is concerned with seeking improvement in the state of the business within its stated objectives. Traditionally, financial planners have been involved in this process by contributing analyses of such things as costing, pricing, investment appraisal and so on, but not always in an integrated way.

There is evidence that this approach may be changing towards linking financial planning with corporate planning. This book formulates a theoretical model of how the links should be attempted.

Finally, there is a critical examination of how the theory has been, or can be, applied to an organisation. Although British Rail's experience is chosen as exemplary material, the conclusions may well be applicable to a large range of other industries in both the public and private sector.

It should also be noted that subsequent to writing the text, changes have occurred that will have a bearing on some of the issues raised. These are summarised in chapter 10.

TWO

Nature and Purpose of Financial Planning

During the last twenty years much has been written about general business planning under many headings, for example corporate planning, long-range planning, corporate strategy, business policy, programming and budgeting systems, financial planning and forecasting. Readers familiar with some of the work in this field may feel that there is a measure of confusion partly because of the non-standard use of terms and their apparent interchangeability.[1] In this chapter we will attempt to shed some light on this area and relate our chosen terms to others in frequent use. We have already noted in the introduction that, in practice, there is an intimate relationship between corporate and financial planning, yet many texts deal with corporate planning and financial planning as if they were entirely separate issues, often mentioning one without the other. In this text, the view is taken that not only does a link exist but that it ought to exist. Thus, much of this chapter is devoted to exploring issues in financial planning undertaken within a corporate planning context. Finally, this chapter will consider the use of computer models in the fields of corporate/financial planning, which are becoming of increasing importance.

2.1 Corporate planning theory

A growing number of companies and other organisations are becoming involved in formal planning activities. These have taken many forms, but the one that seems to be gaining most recognition is based on the concepts and ideas developed in corporate planning. It is not the purpose of this book to examine corporate planning in depth. Rather, it is to consider its major characteristics and examine these in relation to financial planning.

Irrespective of the style, or with whatever success an organisation is managed, the processes involved require that decisions have to be taken. The number and nature of the decisions in an organisation will depend on a large number of factors and decision-takers may be subject to many influences. Many of these influences are from outside the organisation and represent the interaction of the organisation with the environment. Others are from within and relate to the people involved and often to the organisation structures within which they operate. It is not practical or necessary to list all the influences and place them in order of importance because there are far too many and their importance relates to individual circumstances. Indeed, it is unlikely that they are all known. However, to illustrate the complexity of the management decision process, we have attempted to draw an influence diagram in connection with a planning decision (fig. 2.1). The precise nature of the decision is not really important. It may be a fundamental strategic decision or a medium-size investment decision. The important issues are the number of likely influences and their complex changing and interacting relationships.

In this diagram it can be seen that making a planning decision may be an extremely complex task. Let us assume that the decision is whether or not to market a new product, thus adding to the range already provided. The two prime influences are the profitability of the product and the market potential, both requiring forecasts. The other influences contribute, in varying degrees, not just to the two prime influences but to each other. The decision-maker has to consider each in turn and together, giving each the relative importance considered suitable. This can be a daunting task because there is no apparent methodology designed to ensure that the decision is properly placed alongside other related decisions or which gives some influences more weight than others.

No attempt has been made to make the diagram complete, but it serves to illustrate that the number of influences and their interaction is such that a great deal of thought and effort may be necessary to sort and evaluate those which apply, or should apply, in any set of circumstances. To compound the situation, the strength and number of the influences will depend upon the nature of the decision from minor to major, short-term to long-term and the levels of risk and uncertainty involved. As others have argued,[2] this points to the impossibility of arriving at a 'perfect' decision, even if any two people were to agree on what constitutes perfection.

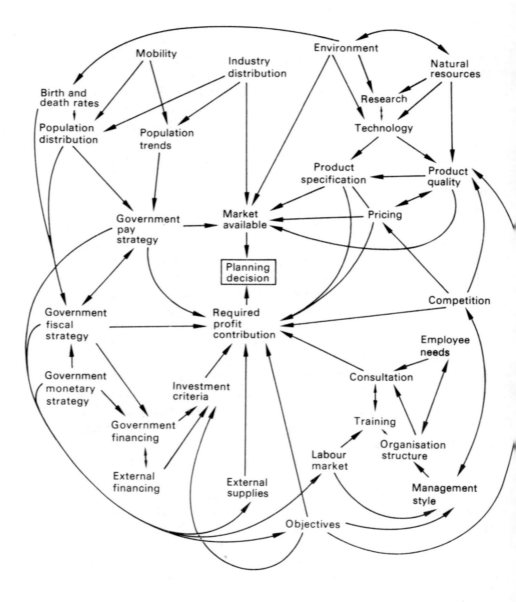

Fig. 2.1 Influence diagram–planning decision

Yet many people have tried to develop techniques and methodologies in an attempt to ensure, if not the perfect decision, much improved decision-making. Examples of these attempts are decision theory, investment appraisal using discounted cash flow (D.C.F.), work study, simulation, linear programming, network analysis and a host of others. It is generally felt that such attempts have been largely piecemeal, mainly because they were developed to deal with particular aspects of particular problems. More and more, decision-makers have become concerned with relating to broader planning issues for the total organisation by identifying selected key variables.

This broader approach is often identified by the title corporate planning. We acknowledge that other names may be used to describe such an approach. We acknowledge also that other activities could be listed under the title of corporate planning. This text will not attempt to be comprehensive in the sense of attempting to cover every conceivable aspect of corporate planning. Instead, it will define corporate planning in general terms and in ways that are particularly relevant to issues in financial planning and hence to the problems of financial planners. In this respect, it is important to note that corporate planning is more than a technique, it is a 'way of management' which attempts to recognise influences and produce a concerted and coordinated approach to management and to the decision-taking process which it requires.

There are many ways through which this may be attempted. Fig. 2.2 provides a model of just one approach, but one which we believe to show most of the characteristics of the corporate planning process. Ideally, a model of the corporate planning process should exhibit a number of major characteristics. First, it should demonstrate the all-embracing nature of the corporate planning process. Second, it should be the 'master plan' which guides all corporate activity. Third, it should provide a mechanism for dealing with, as far as possible, the influences given in the diagram in fig. 2.1 and any others that might apply. This process involves rationalisations which allow identification of the fundamental influences and their weights surrounding planning issues. Moreover, for the approach associated with this model to have any chance of success, two further characteristics are required. The model must be concerned with real issues and there must be full commitment by management regarding the processes and mechanisms of resolving these issues. Let us proceed with an examination of the various stages in the model, with these matters in mind.

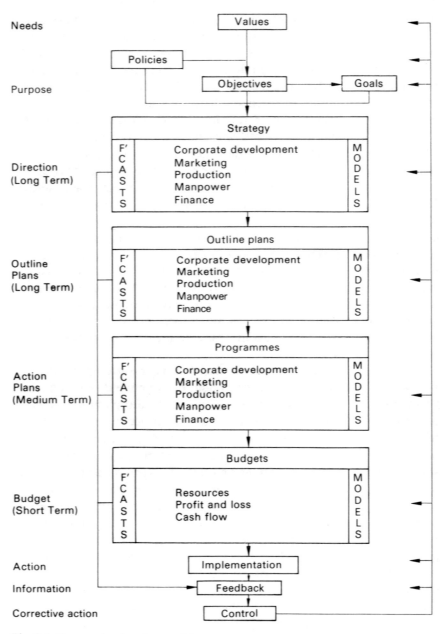

Fig. 2.2 Corporate planning model

It will be seen that the model starts with the determination of the 'needs' of an organisation, which manifest themselves in the shape of the 'values' which may have taken a long time to evolve. These values may be extremely varied in nature and cover a host of items which suit the requirements of the organisation. For example, it may develop a fairly clear-cut social and environmental philosophy which is linked to attitudes towards product quality, service, location of markets, disposition towards external rules and regulations, employment of manpower, use of materials, environmental pollution and many other matters. Further examples of values may be disposition towards change, survival consciousness and attitudes towards growth rates, market position, technical innovation and financial gearing.

In a non-public organisation, these values will be influenced mainly by those of its top management, shareholders, employees, customers and government. As the power balance between these sections changes, so will the values of the organisation change. In nationalised industries and other public organisations, the nature of the influences is similar but government apparently has more influence and top management less. In these circumstances values are often partially imposed by rules and regulations which reflect the values of another tier of management (i.e. the Cabinet) which equally often have fundamentally different motives, aspirations and timescales to those of commercial organisations or indeed the boards of the nationalised industries.

The values attempt to sum up the major influences and set a consistent pattern of response to them. In an ideal world, it would be obvious that this would be dealt with at the outset because the response is critical to the further elements of the model in fig. 2.2. Because every step of the model is subject to a large number of the influences, the key issue would be to sort out and weight the major influences at this point into the summary of values which then become guiding principles. This aggregation of values is not easy. Even in theoretical terms, there are difficult conceptual problems which relate to the quantification and comparison of qualitative variables such as ambition and emotions. In the practical world this is further complicated by the political processes that either explicitly or implicitly, openly or covertly, affect the determination of values. However, irrespective of the method by which they are determined or whether they are expressed in formal or informal terms, these values are a necessary pre-requisite for the determination of 'policies' and 'objectives'. Moreover, there can be little doubt about their existence if 'objective setting' is undertaken in an explicit or non-explicit form. They represent the culture of the organisation and the overall response to the question 'what business are we in'. They relate fundamentally to the management style and are often the result of an evolutionary process. In practice, values held are usually implicit rather than explicit, but because we are discussing what ought to be as opposed to what is, the decision-maker should strive to make them more explicit. This eases the conceptual problems of measurement and comparison, and facilitates the development of a questioning approach which is important in corporate planning.

Following the steps in the model in fig. 2.2, we proceed to the term 'policies', which may be defined as a set of ethical rules and regulations which are based on the values and act as a set of constraints on and basic indicators for, the objectives in part, and the strategy in particular. Like the values, the policies will be quite varied in nature and may cover in considerable detail attitudes towards such matters as growth processes, capitalisation, quality of product and service, employment in a particular area, strict ethical codes of practice, obedience to the laws of any country, trade union membership, marketing in a particular area, safety and advertising. It may be considered from this explanation that the policies are merely a repetition of the values. Indeed, to some extent they are, but there are distinct differences. Values provide the overall scale of measurement and policies provide point estimates where the values are capable of quantification. Furthermore, policies may provide detailed analyses of the vital constraints and appropriate indicators for the business. Even in a formal corporate planning environment, values and policies may be more often implicit than explicit but, ideally, they should be the latter because implementation is largely dependent upon the understanding of those responsible for the achievement of the 'objectives'.

This is even more necessary in the determination of 'objectives' which has been described in the model in fig. 2.2 as the 'purpose' of the organisation. The expression of objectives allows the conversion of the values and policies into concrete anticipated end results. Objectives should not be pious hopes but represent the expected attainment level, given the strategy and 'outline plans' which follow and the level of ambition created at the values and policies stages. They should be fairly long-term and may cover ten years, fifteen years or even longer if considered necessary. Most organisations would consider fifteen years more than adequate bearing in mind that, as will be seen later, corporate planning is an ongoing process. However, the length of time is best determined by the nature of the main assets employed and, in particular, their expected useful life. Thus, for example, a bus operator renewing his fleet every five to eight years may be happy to look ten years ahead. On the other hand, a manufacturer of petroleum products requiring heavy investment in refinery plant might require a much longer term view to justify the potential of his prime investment.

Many authors describe objectives in purely financial terms[3] and in the shape of such outcomes as return on investment (e.g. on assets employed), return on capital employed (e.g. on assets minus short-term liabilities), absolute level of profits, absolute value of assets, earnings per share or level of dividend. These issues are very important and one or more financial objectives will certainly be chosen as part of the total package of objectives for any organisation. However, we would argue that corporate planning is incomplete with financial objectives alone. The objectives of an organisation should embrace other facets of the needs, as relevant, and be as specific as possible in the form of a list of anticipated outcomes covering all key issues. These might include various outcomes such as financial (usually more than one), market share and distribution, product/service quality and distribution, manpower and employee satisfaction, technical innovation, social and environmental considerations and corporate image.

It is unusual to see a description of corporate planning which places a heavy emphasis on the need for non-financial objectives. We consider it necessary to emphasise this issue, not only because we consider it correct to do so but because it is fundamental to our description of financial planning which follows later. Indeed, we would go so far as to say that organisations undertaking corporate planning with financial objectives alone are really dealing with financial planning in a corporate manner. In addition it is as well to note that during the last ten years or so, public and government pressure has tended to make organisations more aware of their wider social responsibilities and has created the growing demand that they become more accountable for their actions. Some of this pressure has produced legal constraints such as the *Race Relations Act, Equal Pay Act, Employment Protection Act* and various measures covering environmental pollution. These add to the need for the development of non-financial objectives, rather than merely regarding them as constraints working against the financial objectives or necessary conditions of financial achievement.

In a non-public organisation, the objectives will be set by the top management in line with their values and policies and the outside influences mentioned earlier. In a public organisation, including the nationalised industries, there may be laid-down objectives which result from rather selective laid-down values. More likely, however, there will be a minimum financial objective coupled perhaps, but more often without, a minimum product/service objective. However, some discretion usually remains with the top management, who can thus expand or extend the objectives, as they consider necessary, but again as influenced by government departments.

The model in fig. 2.2 describes the next stage as the determination of 'goals'. The goals of an organisation need to be absolutely specific and represent a quantified subdivision of the objectives, usually in the form of a set of targets involving numbers and dates. As such they are 'marker points' on the road to the objectives and are needed to assess progress at every level which follows. The choice of goals needs to be undertaken with considerable care and realism because they are often crucial to determining the suitability of the objectives. Most objectives can be subdivided into goals and every effort should be made to ensure that this occurs. However, it is appreciated that there might be some objectives which do not lend themselves to this sort of quantification. This might be the case for example in the area of social objectives. It is important to make such aspirations as explicit and tangible as possible. However, it must be noted at this stage that, in describing the theory of corporate planning, the terms objectives and goals are sometimes given opposite meanings in other texts.

The most difficult area of the model follows and that relates to the determination of 'strategy'. The term strategy denotes the direction in which action should be taken to achieve the objectives and the intermediate goals. Thus it represents the 'means' to achieve the objectives which become the 'ends'. Strategy sets the direction in which the organisation will grow and develop (or decline). In itself, it results in no action. That depends on the 'plans' that follow. It has been described by Ansoff as 'decision making rules for the guidance of organisational behaviour',[4] thus providing a unifying theme for all activities. This definition is very much in line with the model given in fig. 2.2.

It has been mentioned earlier that strategy is heavily influenced by the policies (which are themselves based on the values) and also on the objectives. These influences control the nature of the strategic thought and effort. There can be few organisations sufficiently uninhibited to follow the theories of strategy formulation such as those prescribed by Ansoff, but it does provide a theoretical framework through which the process may be begun. For example, Ansoff's strategy formulation is accomplished through a 'cascade' approach to 'gap closure' formulated in 'gross terms' at the outset and then successively refined.[5] This means that the gap between the aspired results (i.e. related to objectives) and the currently anticipated results (i.e. related to future expected results of current plans and activities) is looked at on a broad and estimated basis. At the outset, theoretically, every conceivable solution is considered and then refined in the light of its contribution to the objectives and acceptability within the values and policies. This approach is intended to produce the best possible solution and not merely the first reasonable strategy to emerge. It is based on the assumption that the objectives are as far-reaching as the values and the policies will allow. In Ansoff's terms, it is also based on financial objectives alone.

This degree of objectivity and intensity of approach is, of course, unrealistic in any organisation. The human factor is bound to intervene with all the accompanying pressures, prejudices, short cuts, 'satisficing' and general tendencies to be as practical and political as possible at every procedural stage. We do not wish to detract, however, from the Ansoff approach and would merely make the case for a considerable amount of effort and endeavour to be applied at the strategy stage, in order that the sense of direction is likely to be the best possible to achieve the objectives. After all, the stakes can be high when the strategy is related to matters under the first general heading within the strategy section of our model, i.e. corporate development.

This element of the strategy represents the starting point which helps decide major aspects of the other elements. It covers the key decisions about such matters as product selection, research and development, make or buy, capital gearing, property ownership and market outlets. These may in turn lead to decisions on acquisition, divestment, diversification, horizontal integration, vertical integration and many other possibilities. Such decisions are very difficult to make and require a level of resolve which should only be marshalled in the light of a searching analysis of values and policies, and with certainty of intentions as expressed through objectives. It is a heart-searching process which demands a knowledge of the competitive situation present and future (as far as possible) and the distinctive competence, 'organisational slack',[6] strengths and weaknesses and potential of the organisation. Every organisation 'learns' and develops its distinctive competence. The successful organisations maintain the development and maximise the benefits from that competence.

The marketing element of the strategy might be expected to follow on logically from the corporate development and go into detail on the marketing strategic issues. These would normally include the strategic elements of market research, selling, advertising, pricing, product research and development, product quality, product distribution and service and marketing control systems. The corporate development element over and above this would set the scene on such an issue as diversification through acquisition. This would still leave the above key marketing issues undecided. The marketing element would also include a prescribed investment requirement.

The production element would be similar, covering the strategic aspects of the manufacturing or service process, maintenance, research and development, utilisation of resources and related control systems. Here again, the production element would also include a prescribed investment requirement which might be critical in creating the ability to match production potential with marketing proposals.

The manpower element of the strategy would be expected to cover the strategic aspects of employment including such things as the skills required, productivity levels, training, pay levels, conditions of employment and manpower control systems. Together with the investment required for production, this could be the most critical issue demanding an exhaustive examination of labour supply, demand and skills. This in turn could make demands on management development and staff training, both features which could make or break the overall strategy. Again, the manpower element might demand a level of investment.

The finance element of the strategy is also a partial summary of the effects of the other elements because each has a cost or a benefit. However, it also relates to the strategic aspects of capital supply, cash flow maintenance and financial control systems. In regard to investment, it is an aggregation process and one of the means by which success is measured because investment appraisal techniques would probably be applied, at least for the major investment proposals.

It is important to realise that these elements are completely inter-dependent. Whilst described as strategic elements, they only become the true corporate strategy when they are put together in the common cause, i.e. the achievement of a set of corporate objectives. The main process for ensuring compatibility is the preparation of strategic forecasts that link the elements by relating the physical and financial figures one with another. This strategic forecasting is best undertaken in fairly broad terms, for ten, fifteen or more years ahead according to the nature and duration of the objectives, with more detailed forecasts being prepared at later stages in the model.

Having determined the sense of direction in an ideal situation, the next stage in the model in fig. 2.2 would be the preparation of 'outline plans' which convert the strategic decisions into approximate actions and consequences. These should be long-term also, but be more refined in the earlier years to correspond with the later stages of the model. The elements of the plans are the same as for strategy formulation and the interdependability of them would be equally crucial. The process of developing outline plans is also certain to involve the use of forecasting procedures. These will be discussed in the next chapter, but it is important to note at this stage that whatever forecasting techniques are used, they are likely to provide fairly general data regarding the future social, political and economic environment. Moreover, they are likely to be 'broad brush' in nature. They might cover a period of between ten and fifteen years in line with, or within the time-scale of, the strategy. Their content would be in the shape of anticipated yearly or year-end position statements, assuming a staged implementation of the strategy, but with only their broad outline—not the precise details of the year-to-year actions—having been established.

These outline plans would provide the basis for the more detailed 'action plans' or 'programmes' which are relatively firm proposals covering a shorter time-scale and not broad statements of intent. Indeed, whilst outline plans might be described as answering the question 'what could we reasonably achieve within the strategy', the action plan would be concerned with making a series of medium-term choices relating to what should be done at this tactical level and, moreover, determining appropriate courses of action through which this may be achieved. These courses of action will also involve forecasts for about three to five or even as much as ten years ahead. The information contained within these action plans should be in considerable detail to ensure that there is no doubt as to their timing or what is intended of them.

It is usual that outline plans would provide broad common guidelines for planners, within the appropriate functional breakdown within the organisation. These guidelines would in turn be used to determine action plans and budgets separately within the functional areas. Hence there is considerable functionalisation of planning at this level. However, it should be noted that, almost invariably, planners have dual responsibilities. They have responsibilty to their functional departments and also to the group co-ordinating the total planning process. This latter responsibility may be formal or informal and arranged through committees or other vehicles as thought appropriate. This functionalisation is sometimes known as the modular approach which will be discussed in more detail in chapter 3 in the section devoted to forecasting.

Moving further down the model, it is necessary for the budgets stage to represent a commitment to the first year of the action plans agreed at all management levels. This process requires the establishment of separate budgets for resources, profit and loss and cash flow within each functional department and below, which itself requires substantial negotiation. This interface between action plans and budgets is important because it represents a change of flow within the planning process. Whereas the earlier stages of the model are generally a headquarters activity, the budgeting stage intimately involves managers at all levels. Moreover the budgeting stage requires information being built up from the lowest levels of the organisation. This 'bottom-up' approach may be contrasted to the 'top-down' approach of stages of the model previous to the budgeting stage.

The model in fig. 2.2 is completed by the inclusion of 'implementation' procedures, 'feedback' processes and 'control' measures. The term implementation is self-explanatory but the others require some comment. The feedback process implies the generation of information concerning the success of the implementation measured in the light of all the previous stages, so that corrective action may, if necessary, be taken. Control means taking the corrective action required by receipt of this knowledge which may require that action be taken at any one, or a combination, of the earlier stages. Feedback and control measures would, in an ideal world, be automatically generated and based on a continuous supply of information.

Indeed, the continuous nature of planning is recognised in the model. This is achieved by using a 'rolling' system frequently updating the forecasts. Furthermore, the interactive nature of planning is explicitly recognised in the model by assuming that each 'box' within the model may react on one preceding it, and others, and require their revision. For example, if a strategy cannot be found to meet objectives, then some change in the objectives may be necessary. The arrows in the model identify this process. Taking the example just mentioned, the arrow leading from strategy direct to feedback would be the route taken if such a situation arose. This in turn might lead to a reassessment of the objectives, values or policies of the organisation. The process by which this interaction is resolved can be exceedingly complex, relying on a mixture of psychological and political motives that determine the power balance within an organisation. Even in a normative model it would be foolish to suggest an 'ideal' route based on a simplistic view of organisations. This implies that feedback processes too can be informal and, with control mechanisms, should not be confined to measuring budget variations, but also strategic, outline plan and action plan variations.

Many corporate planning models assume that the most important planning influences are considered at the values stage and converted into policies which together guide the objective setting and strategy determination. Some influences come, however, into the reckoning much lower down the chain, the weight of each varying according to the stage and the particular circumstances within each stage. Part of the rationale of corporate planning models is to ensure that this 'creaming-off' of the major influences takes place at the values/policies stages, thus ensuring a central view as far as possible.

Corporate planning in the context developed in this section is multi-dimensional. In terms of the model shown in fig. 2.2, it involves the setting of far-reaching objectives, guiding strategies and explicit tactics to meet agreed targets. Each of these involves processes that are overwhelmingly non-mechanical but based on a plethora of influences that are not readily obvious because they involve people's feelings, as well as information based on data. Moreover, these feelings are not always openly expressed. It may be clear that considerable political and psychological skills have to be exercised in relation to the determination of corporate plans. If this were a book on corporate planning we would need to consider these in some detail. It has been emphasised, however, that this book is mainly concerned with examining financial planning–but within a corporate

planning framework. Before moving on to financial planning, however, we would like to stress and distinguish between the need to
establish corporate planning processes and corporate planning mechanisms. What we have so far discussed can be described largely as
processes. The mechanisms can involve planning committees, forecasting techniques, appraisal techniques, all related to the modular
approach which has been mentioned. It should be clear from what has
been said that all functional levels of management ought to be involved
in the corporate planning process. There is an upward and downward
involvement between stages with the senior management only being
involved ideally in the strategy and outline plans, but other management levels being involved with them in the determination of budgets
and perhaps action plans.

It is tempting to imply from this explanation that corporate planning is the sum of financial planning, manpower planning, production
planning, etc. It is certainly this but also much more, particularly with
respect to the harnessing of these aspects. Corporate planning is
designed to produce a state of compatibility and combined purpose
which creates a synergy-like situation from which benefits are accrued
in addition to the sum of the benefits derived from the individual
parts. The methods by which these activities may be co-ordinated has
exercised the minds of many writers and managers. This co-ordination is
sometimes achieved by setting up a small corporate planning department
perhaps responding to a planning director or to a managing director (or
similar). This is often a practical measure, recognising the vast amount
of paper work which is necessary and the need to ensure there is a
pertinent, objective co-ordinating force, separate from line management. The role of such a department needs to be clearly defined so
that responsibility is not taken from the functional departments but
which actively encourages and co-ordinates a modular approach. This
is particularly important if parts of the corporate planning procedures
are computerised. If a team of corporate planners is created, it may be
useful for one or more of its members to have a financial background.
This is not to beat the system by undertaking financial evaluations
outside of the finance department but merely to reorganise the importance of the financial aspects of the corporate planning model.

2.2 Financial planning theory

Given the broad explanation of corporate planning just provided, what then is financial planning? The literature on the broader nature of this subject is somewhat sparse, and there has been little attempt to bring together that which exists. The emphasis has been mostly on the exposition of financial planning techniques and not the development of overall theories. Only since the advent of literature on corporate planning has an overview of financial planning been taken to any significant extent and then with a corporate planning bias, without explanation of the links between corporate and financial planning. We will attempt to put financial planning in perspective before looking at its many facets.

There are two main reasons for describing the main concepts of corporate planning theory in advance of those of financial planning theory. First, we consider that financial planning is an element of corporate planning and second because an understanding of the model in fig. 2.2 makes the task of explanation of the nature and role of financial planning much easier. Indeed, a working definition of financial planning might be that it is the sum of the financial elements of each stage of the model. This does not mean only the stages where the word 'finance' is specifically mentioned in one of the boxes, but all of the stages, because each has a strong financial element. Likewise, manpower planning could be defined in a similar manner as the sum of the manpower elements of each stage. It may be clear from this, but it is certainly clear from empirical and research evidence that financial planning is one of the most important aspects of corporate planning. This partly explains why corporate planning in some organisations is often handled by finance personnel.

A further and fundamental explanation is that many organisations pursue financial objectives only and their financial planning is, therefore, their entire corporate planning. This is probably the most important area of confusion. As we mentioned earlier, many textbooks on corporate planning make the assumption that corporate planning processes should be geared to the determination and achievement of financial objectives only. The word corporate in this sense means that a corporate view is taken of the planning process to prevent sub-optimisation. We would define this as financial planning, no more no less. Yet in some of these same texts, financial planning is seen to be something different and concerned with the mechanics of techniques such as budgeting and with provision of capital.

However, in our view there is a difference between corporate and financial planning. The former must be concerned with non-financial as well as financial objectives and is thus broader in outlook than financial planning. Because most of the objectives used by organisations are financial, then it is clear that there is a considerable overlap between the two. Indeed, in many organisations the main purpose of planning is the achievement of a financial outcome, i.e. financial planning is the prime concern and the evaluation of non-financial objectives is an important but secondary activity. Where there are financial objectives alone, then the model in fig. 2.2 becomes a financial planning model with all of the other elements taking a supportive role only.

Table 2.1   Some of the management techniques which may be used within the four central stages of the corporate planning model

Stage	*Technique*
Strategy	Forecasting (scenario building)
	Simulation
	Costing
	Risk analysis
Plans	Forecasting
	Investment appraisal (major projects)
	Costing
	Simulation
	Cost–benefit analysis
	Risk analysis
Programmes	Forecasting
	Investment appraisal
	Costing
	Simulation
	Cost–benefit analysis
	Linear programming
	Dynamic programming
	Work study
Budgets	Budgetary control
	Costing
	Work study

n.b. It should be noted that forecasting is given here as a technique in its own right as a generic heading covering the various techniques which will be dealt with in chapter 3.

The actual process of financial planning takes many forms and encompasses a number of disciplines and techniques, some of which are given in table 2.1 and will be discussed in the next chapter. Each of these has a part to play in various stages of dealing with financial evaluations. These rely largely on forecast outcomes and, for this reason, the term forecasts appears in the strategy, plans, programmes and budgets 'boxes' in the model in fig. 2.2, where forecasts are essential. However, it must be recognised that financial planning requires non-financial forecasting also, to the extent defined in the objectives. In essence, all the financial planning techniques are designed to produce acceptable financial forecasts, and these are also critical to the corporate planning process.

2.3 Corporate models

Before looking at these issues further (in chapter 3), we consider it essential to cover the use of models in financial planning. For many years, financial planners have used particular models such as linear programming to solve particular problems. In the last ten years, however, there has been a move towards the development of 'corporate' models designed to assist with the whole of the corporate and financial planning activity.

As can be seen from the work of Grinyer and Wooller, by far the greatest stride taken in financial planning in recent years has been the use of models and computer models in particular.[7] Effort has been concentrated largely on three stages of our corporate planning model given in fig. 2.2–outline plans, action plans and budgets, particularly relating to the achievement of financial objectives. The procedures involved are not necessarily based on particular mathematical techniques such as linear programming but are more concerned with the computerisation of existing manual forecasting and evaluation practises. This often involves the simplification of complexity through the identification of variables which are within the control of decision-makers and those which are not and the identification of the nature and dimensions of their effect. This is in essence the fundamental nature of model-building. The purpose of model-building in corporate/financial planning is to speed up the forecasting process and examine the options available and likely results of varying planning assumptions. This is not possible without the use of computer models and the simplification of the evaluations which such models require because a lack of time or the need for oversimplification of data would create too large an obstacle to progress.

We have already said that one of the most important aspects of financial planning is forecasting and the nature of forecasting is such that one cannot be accurate. Further aspects of forecasting are that they are time consuming and have to deal with options and variations caused by changing assumptions. The net result of these issues is that the forecasting process is often badly treated, in that time will not allow all of the options and potential variations to be considered. Indeed, it is not unusual for the preparation of an outline plan covering a ten-year period to take as long as from four to six months to complete in a large organisation; all this without considering any options at all, other than the one deemed central or most likely.

Realising the immense market in this area, the computer manufacturers and some of the computer agencies have developed packages covering the three stages of the model which we have identified but notably in the outline plans and budgets stages. The programs involved enable users, on a time-sharing basis usually, to translate their manual processes into key physical and financial variables, each with its discrete consequential effects. For example a real price change of up to X, Y and $Z\%$ would have respectively inverse consequential effects on output of A, B and $C\%$ and on variable costs of P, Q and $R\%$.

The starting point for such a model is either the financial figures for the last current financial year or, for outline plan models, the budget for the current year or next year. All subsequent changes are modelled according to these dependent variables and their consequential effects. There is nothing especially revolutionary about the procedure in terms of difficult mathematics but its use will revolutionise corporate/financial planning because it will release the planners involved from some of the drudgery of their forecasting processes and enable them to spend more time on strategic issues and consideration of options. One unusual effect of computer modelling is that it is being adopted by some organisations who had no particular system of financial planning other than budgeting in existence. Such is the power of electronics and fashion.

Most of the computer models are presently used for the preparation of five-year outline plans (and in some cases related action plans) and one-year budgets. Their main output is, of course, the forecast profit-

and-loss account and balance sheet. In addition, however, there would normally be the analysis of these forecasts into sectors and profit centres, as appropriate, as well as the related physical facts and their distribution. The means of inputting the data required is first by the creation of sub-programs suitable to the organisation involved and second by feeding in the appropriate figures. In both cases the procedure is interactive in that the main computer program is designed to feed questions to the user which require straightforward responses. The usual means of communication is a terminal within the premises of the user with a visual display unit (V.D.U.) and/or teleprinter device. Access to the computer is through usual post office telephone lines.

The computer agencies usually offer related financial planning packages apart from those already mentioned. They describe the overall process as 'corporate modelling' and recommend use of operations research techniques as a means of taking the forecasts a stage further such as performing risk analysis, trend extrapolation or resource optimisation evaluations. The techniques used mainly in this context are simulation, regression and linear programming.

There can be little doubt that the advent of computer corporate models will be a major force in the development of financial planning and, of course, in corporate planning because many non-financial objectives can also be covered by the procedures. What must not happen in the process, however, is for the corporate/financial planning process to be handed over to a small team of experts isolated from the departments who should be responsible. Ideally, the modular approach outlined earlier should apply and is equally consistent with manual and computerised procedures.

THREE

Financial Planning Procedures

Chapter 2 set financial planning in a context which might appear to elevate it to a level almost on a par with corporate planning. This is quite deliberate because we have argued that financial planning is broader in aspect than is conveyed in many texts. Most texts concentrate on financial planning techniques without much regard to general overall theory. As a result they undermine the status of financial planning in an era of more intensive theorising on corporate planning. What has happened is that financial planning has been incorrectly identified by corporate planners as just one of the inputs to their corporate plan when the truth often is that the corporate plan is in fact a financial plan geared to the achievement of financial objectives alone.

However, the more generally recognised aspects of financial planning require considerable comment which will be provided in this chapter. In doing this, we will be more in line with other financial planning texts because we do not disagree with generally accepted theories in this area. We will deal with forecasting first and then proceed to budgeting, aspects of costing and finally investment appraisal. It is appreciated that this list is not necessarily complete, particularly on pricing theory. Because of constraints of space and because many texts[1] cover pricing theory very adequately, we will not discuss this very vital topic in relation to financial planning.

To facilitate the discussion, we will refer back to fig. 2.2, rather than create a separate model to deal with financial planning.

3.1 Forecasting

In a financial planning sense, forecasting means the prediction of future financial results in a form suitable for decision-taking. This will generally include forecasting profit-and-loss and cash flow figures in a considerable amount of detail, e.g. by division, profit centre, product, etc. In a management science sense, it is a process of figure prediction which itself encompasses a number of techniques. Many of these techniques are extremely useful in their own right and may well be used in financial planning.

Which set of techniques will be used and for what purpose will depend on the stage of the planning process and the needs of the organisation. This is partly a question of time-scale where, for example, the amount of detail and accuracy required of a one-year budget would be greater than for a ten-year outline plan. But it is also a question of purpose. In an uncertain world, the purpose of forecasting is clear. It is to unravel some of the complexity that surrounds each business decision so that any general data available become information pertinent to the situation being studied. Wood and Fildes have described forecasting as an attempt to create a bridge that links data we currently have with data that we would like to have but cannot obtain directly.[2] They go on to suggest that the purpose of the forecast is either to accept the forecast future and to make optimal decisions within the framework or, alternatively, to seek to influence the predicted future; that is, to change the forecast future. At once we see that forecasting is not necessarily a collection of statistical techniques as is often thought. Instead, it is a managerial activity concerned with providing information and understanding for decisions and, in so doing, influencing both the decisions and the decision-making processes. This is largely how we should think of it in terms of fig. 2.2.

Over the long term, the nature of the forecasting procedure, whatever it may be in terms of techniques, will be partly concerned with 'scenario building'. The effect of such a procedure will be to provide the organisation with a broad framework through which it will seek to establish, through an examination of its values, policies, objectives and goals, whether or not it wishes to define a strategy so as to fit the predicted scenario, or whether it wishes to define a strategy that attempts to change that scenario. Whichever of these approaches it attempts to follow, the initial influence in the process will have been provided by the scenario. At this level, the future environment, as depicted in the scenario, is a key determinant in the establishment of a strategy. If corporate planning is to mean anything at all, it has to be based on a philosophy of at least considering change; that is, it is not concerned with simply extrapolating long-term trends from historical data. In that the scenario is a key determinant, the organisation can either accept it or seek to change it. However, this is part of the strategic planning process. What is important to notice is that strategy does not influence the scenario at this stage but the scenario most certainly influences the determination of strategy.

Indeed, a three-part process for forecasting could be established for the strategy stage of the model in fig. 2.2. The first is concerned with an assessment of the environment which will exist in the long term, irrespective of the existence of the organisation. This has been described as the scenario. The second stage is the assessment of how the organisation is currently intending to work within that scenario without developing a strategy different from that which exists or is deemed to exist. The third stage is the development of a strategy which is designed to change the scenario, or get the best out of it, or a combination of both. This process will depend heavily on the values, policies, objectives and goals, as previously described.

It is important that, whatever techniques of forecasting are used, the forecasting undertaken over this longer term is appropriate to the needs of the organisation. This is, of course, begging the question in the sense that we know that forecasts are notoriously inaccurate and the longer the time period the more inaccurate they seem to be. However, the importance of forecasting does not necessarily lie in its statistical accuracy but in its contribution to the managerial decision and learning process. Indeed, it could be argued that the only forecasts that are accurate are so because of management action in relation to the original forecast; that is management action forces the outcome to be near to the prediction. This reinforces the argument that forecasting is an integral part of planning procedures.

However, this statement does not go far enough since it does not say how forecasts are an integral part of financial and corporate planning or whether some forms of integration are more appropriate than others. The answer to the first, of course, depends very much on the structure of the organisation that is being discussed. In the schematic presentation of the corporate planning model in fig. 2.2, the importance of forecasting is emphasised at all points in the process. The integration takes place differently at different levels but the general reasoning behind the model suggests that forecasts are integrated both vertically and horizontally. Forecasts used in the strategy stage affect and are affected by forecasts made at subsequent stages. Thus, there is feedback in the system in a vertical direction. In a horizontal direction, we have already noted that the influence of forecasts of the external environment is a key determinant in strategic considerations.

As we move down through outline plans, action plans and budgets the situation changes. At these stages the emphasis with respect to forecasting moves towards the area of investigating the future results of decisions that may be taken within the confines of the strategy. That is, decisions determine the alternatives considered and forecasting is concerned with attempting to quantify the consequences of such decisions.

The nature of the forecasting procedures is likely to change depending on the level being considered within the corporate or financial planning process. At the strategy determination level, it is likely that the forecasts will be naive (in the sense of a lack of statistical sophistication), macro (in the sense of looking at general trends), based on judgement, intuition, flair, but not on extrapolation of hard data. Furthermore, it is unlikely that the techniques used will be concerned with determining, at this stage, any causal relationships. They are more likely to be concerned with drawing broad scenarios of what may be the picture in the distant future so that planners may view the pictures.

As we move down the levels through outline plans, action plans and budgets the nature of the forecasting procedures is changed. At the outline plans level, it may well be that the forecasting procedure will be concerned with attempting to evaluate through a 'what happens if' procedure–an evaluation of the likely outcome if any one of the alternative courses of action takes place. At the action plans level, it may well be that forecasts become more quantitative in nature. Instead of trying to judge among alternatives, the forecasting emphasis might be more concerned with the determination of as precise an evaluation as possible of the selected alternatives. It might also be that forecasting at this stage would be concerned with investigating the relationships that determine the forecast variables. That is, the forecasting methods will be concerned with explanation as well as prediction. By the time that we reach the budgeting stage the forecasts will be used in a control sense, in that they will provide the mechanism by which 'targets' will be achieved. They are negotiated forecasts and they are the basis of detailed management action.

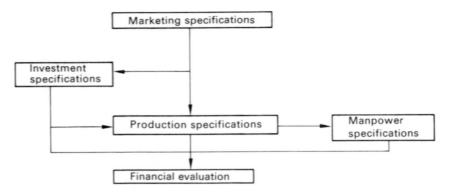

Fig. 3.1 Forecasting process

As far as the middle stages of the corporate/financial planning process are concerned, forecasting involves the production of individual forecasts for each element, the financial forecast being partly in the form of an evaluation. A simplistic view of this process is given in fig. 3.1. This is essentially a modular approach which facilitates the collaboration of the departments of an organisation in the planning–forecasting process. In practice, there might well be considerable overlapping both in content of the specifications and their timing. Thus, the specifications are not likely to be drawn up sequentially, and the order would depend upon the needs and characteristics of the organisation undertaking the forecasting exercise. For the purpose of this section, however, the simple presentation of fig. 3.1 will provide a suitable framework for discussion.

The marketing specification is partly a forecast in itself because it is likely to contain the predicted volumes of sales, product distribution, prices, etc. In brief, it might be an extract from the marketing element of the corporate/financial plan. The method of arriving at the marketing specification will not be dwelt on here except to say that some of the general forecasting techniques to be covered later might well be used. The most important features of the marketing specification are that it specifies sufficient information to enable the investment and production specifications to be prepared. Naturally, this is not a one-way process because it may well be that the marketing specifications may not be acceptable in investment or production terms. The investment specification is the detailed investment requirement necessary to achieve the marketing specification through the medium of changing the production capability. One would almost certainly use the D.C.F. investment and other appraisal techniques in conjunction with some of the forecasts provided in this area. The production specification is likely to take the form of forecast resources requirements (assets and manpower) and the requirements in terms of productivity, inventory, supply, output criteria and resource scheduling. This specification may well require that the investment specification be revised or it may call for a revision of the manpower specification which takes on board such issues as pay, conditions of service, recruitment, training and management development.

Financial planning is partly concerned with the financial evaluation of the other specifications. This is not to say that there is no financial input to the other specifications. The financial evaluation itself is not financial planning, it is only part of the process. However, the financial evaluation may well turn out to be the critical stage requiring changes in one or more of the previous specifications to produce an acceptable forecast. In addition, financial planning will necessarily involve consideration of the implications of independent matters. This is because it has an input of corporate finance issues such as share issues, borrowing and profit retention, and of accounting criteria such as depreciation provisions and accounting for inflation. The main importance of the financial evaluation lies, however in the fact that it provides the means of reconciliation and aggregation of the specifications and of comparison with the other stages of the corporate/financial planning process identified in fig. 2.2. Thus, the routine illustrated in this section is repeated at four stages–strategy, outline plans, action plans and budgets. When put together the overall forecast represents the anticipated end-product of the strategy, outline plans, action plans or budget, as relevant.

It has been emphasised that forecasting is critical to corporate/financial planning and that the type of forecasting differs according to the stage in the process and the time-scales involved, and the relation-ships among the elements of the corporate forecast. In addition, it has been emphasised that the techniques required at each stage will be different because of their different needs. We can now look at the question of techniques a little further. Chambers, Mullick and Smith have classified forecasting techniques into three categories: qualitative methods, time-series analysis and projection methods and causal methods.[3] Examples of each are given in table 3.1. The first category

Table 3.1

Qualitative	Time-series analysis and projection	Causal
Delphi	Moving average	Regression model
Market research	Exponential smoothing	Econometric models
Panel consensus	Box–Jenkins	Intention to buy and anticipation surveys
Visionary forecast	X–11	Input–output model
Historical analogy	Trend projections	Economic input–output model
		Diffusion index
		Leading indicator
		Life-cycle analysis

might be regarded as the 'naive' type which would be concerned heavily with the scenario building part of the planning process. For example, the Delphi technique might be used, through which the forecaster can seek the advice of a panel of experts with respect to likely future scenarios. Unlike a 'brainstorming' exercise the panel makes its predictions dispassionately in the sense that the panelists do not meet. Instead, a questionnaire is usually sent to each of them to be returned to the investigator at the centre, who then combines the information and sends it back out to the panelists to see if they wish to change their views in the light of other experts' considered opinions. This 'to-ing and fro-ing' might go on for a number of rounds.

This is just one example of the naive type of forecasts. The important characteristics of these forecasts are that they do not rely on hard data or extrapolations from the past. Thus they are able to predict 'turning' points more quickly than statistical techniques because they do not assume that what has happened in the past is likely to happen again;

that is, the panelists do not necessarily extrapolate past trends. This type of forecasting is likely to be used in the strategy and outline plan stages of the corporate planning model.

The second category of techniques which are sometimes used rely heavily on extrapolation. They are usually grouped under the general heading of time-series analysis although, as with the naive methods, there are many individual techniques hidden beneath this umbrella title. The important characteristic of these techniques is that they are not so much interested in explanation as in prediction. These types of forecasts are concerned with what the future is likely to be without attempting to explain what management action may be needed to ensure that future. Moreover, the techniques are univariate, this meaning that only one variable is used in the prediction process and this tends to be time. Thus, these techniques rely heavily on the assumption that what has happened before is likely to happen again in almost precisely the same form, in the future. Time-series analysis techniques might be used in the strategy stage but are more likely to be used in later stages of the corporate/financial planning model, particularly the action plan stage.

The final class of forecasts, the causal types, usually involve the use of quite sophisticated statistical procedures. Among the most common of these are those involved with multiple regression techniques. It is not the purpose of this book to get involved in the detail of such techniques but it is important to note that they are normally involved in analysis on a multivariate basis and where hard data are available. It is also important to note that they are involved primarily with establishing the relationships between variables so that management action may be taken in the light of these relationships. Thus, they are concerned with explanation, although, of course, every explanatory model is also a predictive model. Because of the need for explanation, a set of statistical problems can arise and it is important for a financial planner to take the advice of a competent statistician about these problems and how they may be handled. Causal techniques would normally be used in the action plan and budget stages of the model in fig. 2.2 where more hard data would be available.

3.2 Budgeting and budgetary control

Budgeting is one of the most important financial planning processes which is practised widely and often outside of a broader corporate/ financial planning environment. Its use since the Second World War has been almost universal in commercial and industrial undertakings as well as public bodies. Only in the last fifteen years, as a result of the later development of corporate and financial planning, has there been any significant move towards linking budgeting to the broader planning process. However, there is still a tendency to regard budgeting as a discrete process, with corporate/financial planning ending at the outline plan stage.

Anthony and Herslinger state that 'in concept the budgeting process follows, but is separate from the programming process [and] is supposed to be the fine tuning of the programme for a given year, incorporating the final decisions on the amounts to be spent for each part of the programme and making clear who is responsible for carrying out each part of the programme'.[4] We accept this general outline and regard the programme, which we have described as an action plan, as a sort of budget prepared by headquarters for a medium-term period (say five years) which attempts to pre-determine what each of the five annual budgets will look like with a little less accuracy than the budgets themselves. Every key decision will specially feature in the programme covering such items as investment dates and details, reorganisation schemes, marketing campaigns and production changes. It might be described as a comprehensive list of schemes with forecasts of financial and physical end-products attached.

Thus, the budget can be a confirmation of the first year programme forecasts. It is a lot more than this however. It is a fundamental aspect of communication and control. The word 'responsibility' used by Anthony and Herslinger is the key to the process. If we assume that an organisation has prepared an action plan as part of its corporate–financial planning procedures, it would have become necessary for the content of that action plan to be communicated downwards to the levels responsible for implementation.

Budgets must be processed for each responsibility level. The accepted method of achieving this is to start at the bottom and work up to the top. The bottom may be a retail outlet or a part of a factory but it is always a place where costs can be easily collected and considered to be under control of one individual. This is known as a cost centre. It is not necessary for a cost centre to be capable of knowing its receipts. These are collected at receipts centres where one person is again considered to be responsible. In some cases they will be the same.

The budgeting process depends on each responsible person negotiating with his superior on the basis of the expected level of costs, revenues and related resources. This process is repeated up the chain of command in pyramid fashion until headquarters level is reached. The ultimate criteria of acceptability would naturally be the action plan. But it must be remembered that because the budget is likely to contain the greatest amount of pertinent data, the action plan might have to be modified to accommodate the feedback obtained through the budgeting process.

This process is usually designed to produce the resources budget and profit-and-loss budget. It will also normally produce the cash flow budget which brings in such items as borrowing, investment spending and working capital requirements. However, it is likely that the cash flow budget will not be prepared at cost/receipt centre level but either at an intermediate, i.e. divisional level, or at the headquarters level. Many of the items involved are 'spent' at this higher level.

The end result of this process is a fully negotiated budget which matches the action plan, modified by the feedback received. Whilst this is the cornerstone of the overall feedback process, the feedback information must also be able to indicate performance against the action plan, outline plan and strategy to enable corrective action to be taken at the appropriate level. This emphasises that corporate/ financial planning is not a 'once-off' process but a rolling process, updated and modified as events dictate. This is usually taken to be on at least an annual basis.

The methods of arriving at budgeted costs at the lower levels will depend on the organisation and the individuals but it is strongly recommended that it be regarded as a two-part process. The first part of the process is to evaluate the 'standard' level of resources and costs assuming no problems of vacancies, sickness, plant failures, etc. The second stage is the assessment of the 'extras' to allow for the factors that make the standard unattainable. This might involve extrapolation of past data. The purposes of this two-way process are to assist intelligent negotiation of budgets and to facilitate identification of causes of variation during the monitoring procedures.

During the budget preparation process it will be seen that, at various levels, it is pertinent to compare costs with receipts and arrive at a profit before certain centrally controlled charges are identified. This is known as a 'profit contribution' and might well be established at a division, branch or factory level–whatever the appropriate profit centre is deemed to be. Action plans and outline plans (in some organisations) should recognise this and forecast the profit centre results. Such a procedure may well be used as part of a 'management by objectives' system with the budgeted profit contributions being one of the chosen 'objectives'.

It may be considered necessary to create profit centres which do not fall out of the process automatically. For example, if a factory is an automatic profit centre because the factory manager is responsible for receipts and costs which can be compared one with another, it may also be required to establish profit centres for the various products. This may not be possible by merely associating each cost/receipts centre with a product because they may cover more than one product. Instead, it is necessary to subdivide the costs and receipts over the profit centres. On the costs side, at least, this will involve an element of work measurement. Provided the procedures do not involve much arbitrary allocation of costs and receipts, the establishment of such profit centres can be extremely useful. They can represent the best element of the feedback, demonstrating areas which require something more than low level corrective action. The creation of profit centres has been one of the most important advances made in budgeting in the last fifteen years, second only perhaps to the asssociation with broader corporate/financial planning.

3.3 Aspects of costing

In the previous section we mentioned that the establishment of profit centre forecasts and results involves the attribution of receipts and costs to the profit centres. This applies also to groups of profit centres which may be amalgamated to form a product-based division, a factory division, a geographical division or any other sector of the business beneath the board headquarters level which may be considered necessary. This too is a profit centre but is best described as a 'sector'.

This section will take these issues further and be concerned with some aspects of costing, i.e. those that seem most pertinent to consider in context of financial planning as described in this book. We shall not deal with standard costing, marginal costing, fixed and variable costs and other such issues which, although they form part of financial planning, are best dealt with in a textbook on costing. Instead the section will concentrate on an examination of the process of receipts and costs analysis and the problems this creates.

A fundamental requirement of any system of associating receipts and costs to sectors of the business and to the profit centres beneath, is to establish a meaningful distribution of them so that they are useful for the purposes of planning, monitoring and control. To enable all three to be achieved, it is necessary to adopt a realistic stance to the appropriation procedures and not engage in arbitrary arithmetic.

For example, at the profit centre level, it is best to identify, from within the cost centres, only the 'specific' costs (i.e. those which can be directly and solely related to that output) and the specific receipts (this usually means all), thus producing a profit 'contribution'. The sum of the profit contributions of the profit centres would represent the total profit contributions to those costs remaining (offset by any remaining receipts), i.e. those which could not be specifically attributed. Such costs, which should be described as 'joint' costs, would certainly include administration but should also include the cost of shared facilities, where the level of such costs are thought not to vary significantly given the elimination of the output of a sector/ profit centre. These joint costs would include such costs as factory rent, rates and the costs of any other shared facility, including plant and machinery which would not vary to any significant degree if the profit centre did not exist or significantly reduced its output.

It may be appropriate to identify an additional type of cost known as 'common' costs to deal with non-specific expenditure, the shares of which can be clearly identified between one or more sector/profit centres and the total of which would vary according to the level of output. This might apply, for example, to a maintenance department servicing factory machinery, the costs involved being heavily dependent on the level of work. In such circumstances it would be reasonable to appropriate the common costs and add them to the identified specific costs.

A small firm might produce its financial forecasts and results in the form shown in table 3.2. In these circumstances, the proprietor of the firm would have established a realistic assessment of the worth of each profit centre within his factory.

However, in a larger organisation, the factory itself may be a profit centre also but would be described as a sector and, in these circumstances, the profit contribution of the factory would usually reflect the total costs incurred in that factory plus any portion of those incurred

Table 3.2

	£	£
Profit contributions		
(specific revenue minus specific/common costs)		
Profit centre–Product *A*		
B		
C		
D		
E		——
Total		
Deduct joint costs		
Shared facilities		
Administration	——	——
Net profit of factory		══

at a higher level (e.g. at company headquarters) which can be seen to be specific or identified common costs. This will be a completely rational situation which treats all of the costs incurred at the factory as specific costs since at this level they will be. At this level, the costs would not exist if the sector output did not exist since, presumably, the factory would close and the assets be disposed of. Generally speaking, in such a situation the factory manager could be held responsible and account-able for the results of his sector's profit contribution and, within the sector, each profit centre manager held responsible for his profit centre contribution.

Major problems can exist, however, where the circumstances of the sectors are different. Again assuming a medium or large firm, it is quite likely that the sectors will not be based on factories but on products. Let us assume a firm with two products each made in four factories with the directors wishing to establish the profit contribution of each sector. In these circumstances, one would expect to find that there are at least two profit centres in each factory, providing the profit contribution of each product in each factory using specific costs. When combining these to sector level, it is necessary to consider the joint costs to establish whether they can be appropriated to the two sectors. By and large, it will be found that this cannot be done unless one were to resort to an arithmetic allocation of the cost of shared facilities and administration using broad output or throughput statistics.

Such allocations are widespread and sometimes regarded as part of costing and financial planning theory. This is nonsense. It is neither practical nor reasonable to expect a sector manager to be responsible for an allocation of joint costs because he cannot control that allocation. Further, it is not practical to attempt to monitor the results of such allocations against forecasts and expect any form of intelligent feedback at the sector level. Such costs can only be controlled as a whole and not in the form of arbitrarily allocated parts.

Many organisations take this nonsense further and expect their sector managers or even their profit centre managers to be responsible also for an allocation of costs incurred at the headquarters level, the intention being to disperse all costs. They would do the same with any incidental or special receipts which could not be directly associated with each sector. In doing this, the sector managers find themselves being held responsible for costs over which they cannot exercise a reasonable degree of influence. However, we realise that in many organisations the amount of joint costs is relatively small when compared with the specific costs. Generally speaking, the joint costs in these circumstances are mostly administration which may only amount to 5–10% of the total costs. In such circumstances, the need to resort to cost allocation may be considered justifiable to ensure full dispersal of receipts and costs over sectors and the consequent sectoral subdivision of the company's profit or loss.

However, in many other organisations, the level of joint costs is a very high proportion of the total. This renders allocation of joint costs a meaningless exercise. Such situations arise where the administration costs are high and where there is an extensive rundown of one of the sectors. We will see in chapter 6 that British Rail is not only an example of this situation, but the level of joint costs is so high as to make it a prime example.

Where this problem exists, there are only two possibilities which satisfy the test of ensuring that the sector manager and his superiors can use the forecasts and results for planning, monitoring and control. The first has already been covered, namely establishing the profit contribution resulting from applying specific costs to specific revenue and then deducting the remaining costs (less remaining receipts) from the sum of the profit contributions of all sectors at the headquarters level only. This could produce a layout of forecasts and results as shown in table 3.3.

Table 3.3

	£	£
Profit contributions		
(specific revenue minus specific/common costs)		
Sector (product) *A*		
B		
C		
D		——
Total		
Add other receipts		——
Deduct Joint costs		
Shared resources		
Administration	——	——
Net profit of company		——

The other possibility is to move to an 'avoidable' receipts and costs system. In such a system the specific/common and joint costs would be analysed to establish the extent to which they would not exist given the elimination of one of the sectors, each of the others remaining at the present level, or planned level if it were dealing with forecasts. Not surprisingly, it should be discovered that the specific costs are almost wholly avoidable because they are directly and solely related to that output. Common costs would also be largely avoidable. On the other hand, the joint costs will be largely unavoidable. However, it will usually be found that a portion of the joint costs is avoidable because the elimination of that sector would result in a restructuring of facilities and a reorganisation of administration, producing what might be a fairly large cost reduction. It will also be found that some costs are avoidable to more than one sector (i.e. dual avoidability), particularly because of this second-order avoidability approach. This is quite reasonable, although some people might doubt the logic of charging two sectors with the same item of cost.

This procedure would, therefore, produce sector avoidable costs which are greater than the specific costs provided under the first system. These extra costs are quite valid as a charge to the sectors involved since they would not exist if the sector did not exist. They may add little to the concept of monitoring and control compared with the first system in many organisations, but they would permit a greater degree of cost apportionment and therefore profit and loss apportionment which might be valuable for some planning purposes, e.g. where abandonment is being considered.

Where a high degree of joint costs exists the sector profit contributions in the first system have to be examined in the light of their size compared with the remaining unapportioned costs, i.e. the joint costs. In doing so there is a tendency to try to subdivide the joint costs over the sectors to try to measure their share of the net profit or loss. This amounts to unofficial and short-cut recourse to cost allocation, albeit only for testing the strength of the profit contributions. Thus, the main benefit of the second system is that it can significantly decrease the size of the unapportioned costs because they no longer represent the whole of the joint costs. Examination of sectoral profit contributions may be greatly facilitated by the use of avoidable costs, as a consequence of this greater cost apportionment and the related greater understanding of the nature of the joint costs.

However, we must not forget the receipts. If avoidable costs are used, then it follows that avoidable receipts must also be used to establish the avoidable profit contribution. This can produce a very difficult problem in that avoidable receipts are not always easy to determine. In some circumstances a contributory receipts situation exists, i.e. if a sector did not exist then receipts would be forgone in other sectors either because they are directly related or because the customer may choose not to deal with a firm which cannot provide a full enough range of services. In other circumstances, the opposite situation exists in that one or more of the other sectors might benefit from the elimination of a sector. The latter possibility is less likely to exist or be significant and the former will produce the problem, if any, for most organisations. We will observe in chapter 6 the related British Rail implications of operating such a system where the contributory revenue problem is significant.

Under this avoidable approach, the layout of the forecast or results might be like that shown in table 3.4.

Of course, this now begs the question as to whether the avoidable approach can be used in respect of the profit centres within the sectors. We have already seen that under the specific/joint system the sum of the specific costs of the profit centres within a sector is not equal to the specific costs of the sector because what is specific depends on the level of examination. The same applies to profit

Table 3.4

	£	£
'Avoidable' profit contributions (avoidable receipts minus avoidable costs). Sector (product) *A*		
B		
C		
D		——
Total		
Add/deduct Remaining receipts		——
Deduct Remaining costs		——
Net profit of company		——

centres where the sum of the avoidable costs (or receipts) of the individual profit centres is likely to be considerably different from the avoidable costs of the sector. This is not a particular problem because it can be overcome by a general understanding of the concept and efficient layout of profit centre/sector management information. However, what might be a problem is the degree of information and expertise required to determine accurate avoidable receipts and costs at any level lower than the sector level. Over and above this there is the problem of obtaining information regarding the consequential effects of restructuring facilities and/or reorganisation of resources, i.e. the second-order effects.

For this reason, we do not recommend the use of the 'avoidable' system for profit centres. However, we recommend the approach at sector level in cases where the joint costs are high. The main reason for this recommendation is the fact that it is almost impossible to prevent informal allocation of joint costs to test contributions to joint costs. The importance of avoiding arbitrary cost allocations cannot be stressed too greatly and is worth doing a great deal to prevent.

A related, although not core, issue in financial planning is that of transfer pricing. This concerns the price of an item produced by one part of an organisation which is then 'sold' to another part. The transfer price is often difficult to establish and might have a significant effect on profit centre/sector results. The basic rule in this case is that the transfer should take place at current realisable market value.

However, this is often extremely difficult or even impossible to determine because of the nature of the item and the absence of an apparent market. In the circumstances, shadow prices might be considered, which can be obtained through the application of linear programming, in the shape of the 'marginal contributions' that process provides.[5]

To conclude this section, it is useful to stress the broader financial planning implications of what has been said. Referring again to the sections on forecasting and budgeting, it should be readily appreciated that it is vital to provide meaningful information at all of the stages of the model. By and large this will include forecasting profit-and-loss and cash flow figures at every stage and, of course, producing actual results at the 'feedback' stage. The profit-and-loss figures will be most useful if they relate not only to the whole but also to the sectors and profit centres beneath. Indeed, it is likely that sound judgements and comparisons with alternatives could not be made without such information. In a nutshell, therefore, the aspects of costing covered in this section are vital to financial planning and should not be overlooked.

3.4 Investment appraisal and control

Throughout each of the stages of the corporate planning model in fig. 2.2 there would generally be a required level of capital investment. This will usually have a major bearing on the financial planning elements of corporate planning and the effect will be spread throughout the stages, according to the nature and size of the investment projects. For example, if the strategy is one of diversification and this requires major investment, then that investment is an important aspect of the strategy. However, the replacement of a vital and expensive machine with a new and better machine may not be a strategic issue, but could well have a major effect on the outline plan stage. Whatever the effect on the various corporate/financial stages, it is vital that proposed investment schemes are thoroughly prepared to ensure that, as far as possible, they will match the requirements. The process of validating investment proposals is known as 'investment appraisal', which is a major topic in its own right. Because of constraints of space, we will provide an elementary summary of the topic as a whole, concentrating on the more fundamental issues as they relate to financial planning. This will include consideration of the effect of inflation on investment appraisal which is often not covered in other texts. The discussion of risk analysis in the context of financial planning, including investment appraisal, is left until chapter 8.

Naturally, investment appraisal is linked closely with forecasting. Indeed, forecasting forms the primary input to the process which attempts to match expected outlays with expected returns. The accuracy of these forecasts will depend on the skill and effort of those involved in the forecasting as much as the rest of the forecasting requirements of financial planning already discussed. We will not dwell further on this but refer, instead, to an aspect of the theoretical process designed to measure the acceptability of the forecast returns, usually known as 'discounted cash flow'. However, let us start with more basic methods of measuring the acceptability of forecast returns on investment projects. In doing this, it is best to assume that we are dealing with a problem where investment projects have to be ranked to enable the best to be chosen. We shall deal with the question of limited funds a little later.

The most basic method is probably ranking by inspection. This could be used in limited instances where:

(a) two investments have equal cash flows to the end of the life of one with the other continuing for a longer period.

(b) the cash flows over the life of the projects are the same in total but where one produces a bigger net inflow earlier in the life of the project.

The next simple method is the 'pay-back period' method. This involves a simple calculation of the number of years required to pay back the original investment such as that shown in table 3.5. This

Table 3.5

Project	Pay-back period (years)	Ranking
A	6.5	3
B	4.0	2
C	7.5	4
D	3.0	1

method ignores the size of the investment and can, therefore, give misleading results. It also fails to recognise the timing of the cash flows and the value of cash flows after the pay-back date.

A further simple method is to calculate the return on investment by calculating the average book value of the investment and the average annual cash inflow. This provides for the calculation of a return on investment (R.O.I.) percentage. Again, this procedure fails to take into account the timing of the cash flows.

The serious inadequacy of these methods has led to the development of discounted cash flow techniques which take account of the timing of the cash outflows and inflows. Two methods are practised: the yield method and the net present value method. Both will be considered.

Before proceeding, however, it is essential to understand the concept of allowing for the timing of the net cash flows. This is not a method of recognising inflation but, instead, a method of recognising that money received today is worth more than money received a year later because the former can be invested and earn interest in the interval. Therefore, the real question is how much received today is equal to £1 received one year today? Continuing on this basis, the present value of £1000 receivable in five years' time can be defined as that quantity of money required to be invested today at compound interest in order to have £1000 in five years' time.

Investment appraisal on this basis reduces all project cash inflows and outflows to a common present value basis. This recognition of the time value of money has the effect of placing competing projects on an equal footing if every project is reduced to a calculation of its net present value (N.P.V.), i.e. the discounted cash inflows less the discounted cash outflows. The system also provides for a calculation of yield which is that discount percentage which reduces each project to a net present value of zero. The assessment of yield or internal rate of return will frequently lead to the same decision as the calculation of net present value. However, this is not always the case. It must be remembered that the yield is the rate of return on capital invested and not an absolute measure. The absolute size of the investment and the size of the return are often crucial to the decision. For example, it may be more appropriate to invest £10 000 to earn £12 000 in one year's time than £100 to earn £125 in one year's time. In the first case the yield is 20% and in the second 25%, but the circumstances of the organisation and the availability of other projects might require that the first be chosen, despite the lower yield. It is best to calculate both N.P.V. and yield but not use yield where projects are exclusive and where the relative rate of return may not, therefore, be the deciding issue.

A further useful measure which will avoid the problem associated with the yield evaluation is the profitability index. This gives a method of ranking projects for which the N.P.V.s have been assessed, in order of profitability. The profitability index is obtained by dividing the present value of net cash flows by the present value of the amount invested.

However, these procedures beg two important questions. The first is about the rate of discount to be used. The theoretical answer is that it represents the organisation's 'cost of capital' which is usually taken to mean the weighted average related to the different sources of capital used by the organisation. This figure can be the cost of borrowing, recognising the risks associated with the investment or the interest available on lending (on equivalent risk items) if the money is already available, or a combination of both. Suffice it to say that it is a very difficult calculation. Most organisations, including British Rail, use fairly arbitrary percentages and some use an artificially high figure as a safety precaution, sometimes varying according to the perceived level of risk.

The D.C.F. (discounted cash flow) procedure assumes, therefore, that there is a unique 'cost of capital'. On this basis it can be regarded as a profit maximising technique because organisations should undertake every conceivable investment which produces a positive net present value. Of course, most organisations find themselves limited by their objectives and strategy development which would not be as far-reaching as the maximising concept surrounding the D.C.F. approach. Also, it is usual to prepare capital programmes within the strategy (or implicit strategy) thus limiting the investment funds available during the period covered by a financial plan. This process is often described as 'capital rationing', which is part of the action plan and cash flow budgeting procedures mentioned in section 3.2. The D.C.F. process is able to function within that constraint because it is designed to facilitate the choice of best projects. The choice merely becomes more imperative in these circumstances. Indeed, what is best can sometimes be rather difficult to establish where the size of the net present values does not provide an automatic sequencing of projects because of capital budgeting constraints. In such circumstances a second-best sequencing has to be established. This would normally be achieved by inspection but can be established with varying degrees of efficiency through mathematical model building,[6] internal rate of return (i.e. yield) and the profitability index.

The second question concerns the effect of inflation on the cash flows and on the discount rate. In looking at this matter, it must be appreciated that, currently, cost of borrowing will be very high largely because of the high level of inflation which is being experienced. Indeed, this has been the situation for the whole of the 1970s. Consequently, the real rate of interest (i.e. discounting inflation) in recent years has been very low–in the region of 1 or 2% on average and nil in some years. This factor must be given due recognition in the D.C.F. procedures.

There are two ways of dealing with this. One is to use a money rate of return equal to the assessed cost of capital and to forecast future cash flows in future actual prices. The alternative is to use an assessed real rate of return and forecast the future cash flows in true constant prices. Effectively this represents today's price levels, plus and minus the predicted real changes. The real changes would certainly include staff costs where, despite the ups and downs of recent years, there has been an underlying trend of real staff cost increases since the Second World War.

Both systems are difficult but, properly done, they produce the same answer.[7] Both require that an assessment be made of the most difficult feature of all, which is the future rate of general inflation. This also implies an understanding of what can be used as the measure of general inflation. The answer to this depends on the nature of the organisation but most are happy to use the retail prices index as a reasonable proxy.

To summarise, we consider that investment appraisal using the D.C.F. technique is essential to the success of financial planning. It should be used extensively at the outline plans and programmes stages and, as relevant, at the strategy stage of our model in fig. 2.2. However, appraisal alone is not sufficient and questions of control must be considered. It would be inadequate to conduct a comprehensive financial appraisal at the outset only to find that the actual outlay was much higher or the benefits were much lower.

Control over the outlay is best achieved by a project monitoring report, perhaps prepared on a monthly basis. Such a report should record the actual and budgeted expenditure to date and give an up-to-date estimate of the final outlay. Such information is essential to ensure that all important changes are observed and corrective action taken. This action might involve a variation in the project and the preparation of a fresh investment appraisal.

Control over the benefits is, in some respects, more difficult in that these may not arise until the project is complete and may in any case be difficult to identify separately. The most frequently used method is to include the predicted benefits in the budget and monitor budget variations as accurately as possible, identifying the investment project items (separately or jointly) as far as possible as a separate cause of change. Cost reductions are relatively easy to identify, but increases in receipts may arise from a variety of causes which cannot be separately assessed. Some judgement is often necessary in analysing the causes of changes in receipts.

FOUR

British Rail–Nature of Business

The intention of this chapter and chapter 5 is to provide information about British Rail. It is not intended to delve too far back into the past since this would not be relevant and, in any case, various 'railway historians' have produced a good deal of written material in this area. Instead, the comments will be confined to the existing position and reflect on some of the changes since the early sixties. The purpose of this information is to provide a context for the later chapters that will use British Rail as the case study to consider financial planning issues. This chapter concentrates on the nature and size of the business. The financial situation is dealt with in chapter 5.

British Rail is a large and important nationalised industry which has seen halcyon days, is slowly adapting itself to environmental change and has a future which is not certain but has become less uncertain since about 1976. It is not one business but many, all coming under the umbrella of the British Railways Board, the B.R.B. The term 'British Rail' represents the corporate title of the many businesses managed by the British Railways Board. The entire complex is a very large and varied business. It is one of the largest employers in the United Kingdom; it employed just over 243 000 people at the end of 1978, which represented about 1% of the United Kingdom labour force.

The main businesses within British Rail are

Railways
British Rail Engineering Ltd (BREL)
British Transport Hotels Ltd (BTH)
British Railways Property Board
Sealink (U.K.) Ltd

55

British Rail Hovercraft Ltd
Transportation Systems and Market Research Ltd (Transmark)
Freightliners Ltd

The British Railways Board, which was created on 1 January 1963, is charged with the responsibility of running British Rail. The main organisational structure is given in fig. 4.1, where it can be seen that the boards of the businesses are responsible to B.R.B. This they do through their managing directors or equivalent, in the case of those which are not limited companies. The chairman of each non-railways business is always a full-time board member of the B.R.B. The chief executive of the Railways Business is a full-time board member. He is responsible for the general managers of the five geographical railways regions. In November 1979 there were eight full-time and six part-time members of the British Railways Board. The chairman is one of the full-time members and each of the remaining full-time members has executive responsibility. The board membership responsibility structure was changed in January 1977 (previously it was a board on which no member had executive responsibility). The board is responsible to the Secretary of State for Transport. The Secretary of State for Transport appoints all board members including the part-time members, who do not represent any of the special interests such as government, trade unions, etc.

There are a number of other organisations above British Rail to which the B.R.B. owes a measure of responsibility and some of these are given in fig. 4.2. Some of these will be dealt with in more depth later when particular issues are discussed. It is clear, however, that the B.R.B. does not work in an independent manner. The controls over its operations are considerable and stem in the main from the organisations given in fig. 4.2. The relationships with these other organisations are complex and related to individual aspects of running the business. In theory, contact with central government departments is via the Secretary of State for the Department of Transport, but in practice direct contact at lower levels frequently occurs. The board's prime and legal responsibility is to the Secretary of State for the Department of Transport, and this department is the means for contact with other central government departments. The Department of Transport has responsibilities with respect to establishing objectives, policy guidelines, strategy approval, plan approval, major investment approval and monitoring of the performance of these.

The Secretary of State is in turn responsible to the Cabinet and Parliament to ensure that the board manages its business in line with

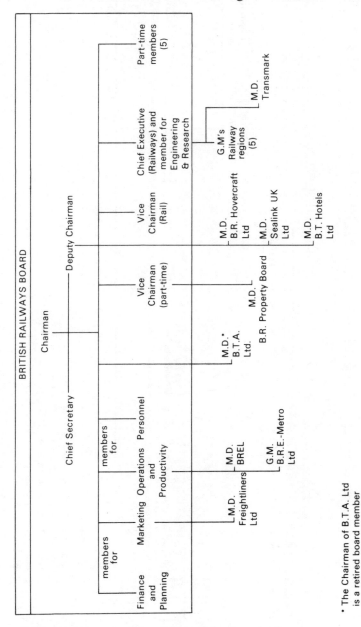

Fig. 4.1 British Railways: board members and main activities

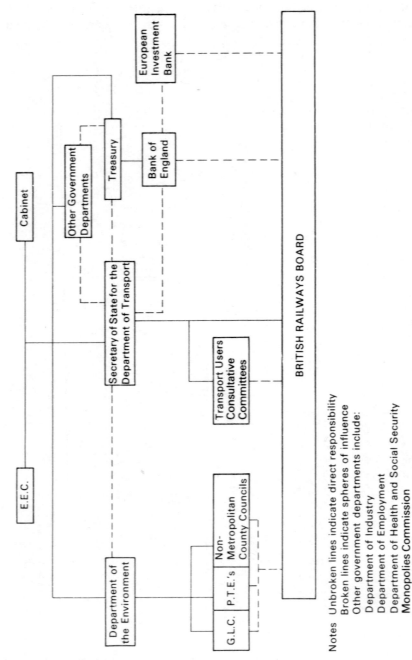

Notes Unbroken lines indicate direct responsibility
       Broken lines indicate spheres of influence
       Other government departments include:
       Department of Industry
       Department of Employment
       Department of Health and Social Security
       Monopolies Commission

Fig. 4.2 British Railways Board: main relationships with government

statutes and directives. The board is not autonomous as is that of an ordinary public company. The statutes and directives represent major disciplines and constraints, much of which would be present even if British Rail were in a profit-making situation.

The individual businesses within British Rail are self-accounting but are not autonomous. They are analogous to divisions in a large company. They make decisions concerning the day-to-day running of the businesses and the implementation of strategy but have no independence in matters of a strategic nature or in respect of large investment (i.e. in corporate planning). Indeed, there is a high degree of central control over all strategic decisions. The extent of the involvement of each business and the regions of the railways business is discussed in detail in chapter 6, but it can be said at this stage that each business plays a large part in the development of its portion of the strategy and that a 'corporate plan' is prepared for each business as well as an overall corporate plan.

The board members exercise their responsibilty through a number of functional chief officers who are in day-to-day contact with railways regional general managers and the managing directors (or equivalent) of the non-railways businesses. They also have links with the functional officers of the railway regions and their equivalents in the other businesses. Details of the chief officer structure are given in fig. 4.3. This chart indicates the relationship with the full-time board members. The part-time board members relate to the chief officers as necessary as, indeed, does each full-time board member in regard to matters outside his direct responsibilty.

The board structure given in figs. 4.1 and 4.3 was created in 1978 and is a little different from that which existed during 1977. The main differences are that the finance member became Member for Finance and Planning with the responsibilty for medium term planning and a new position of Vice-Chairman (Rail) was created to co-ordinate longer term planning.

Having mentioned the businesses and briefly considered the role of the B.R.B. let us now look at each business in turn and isolate the salient features, with the exception of those relating to finance which will be dealt with in chapter 5.

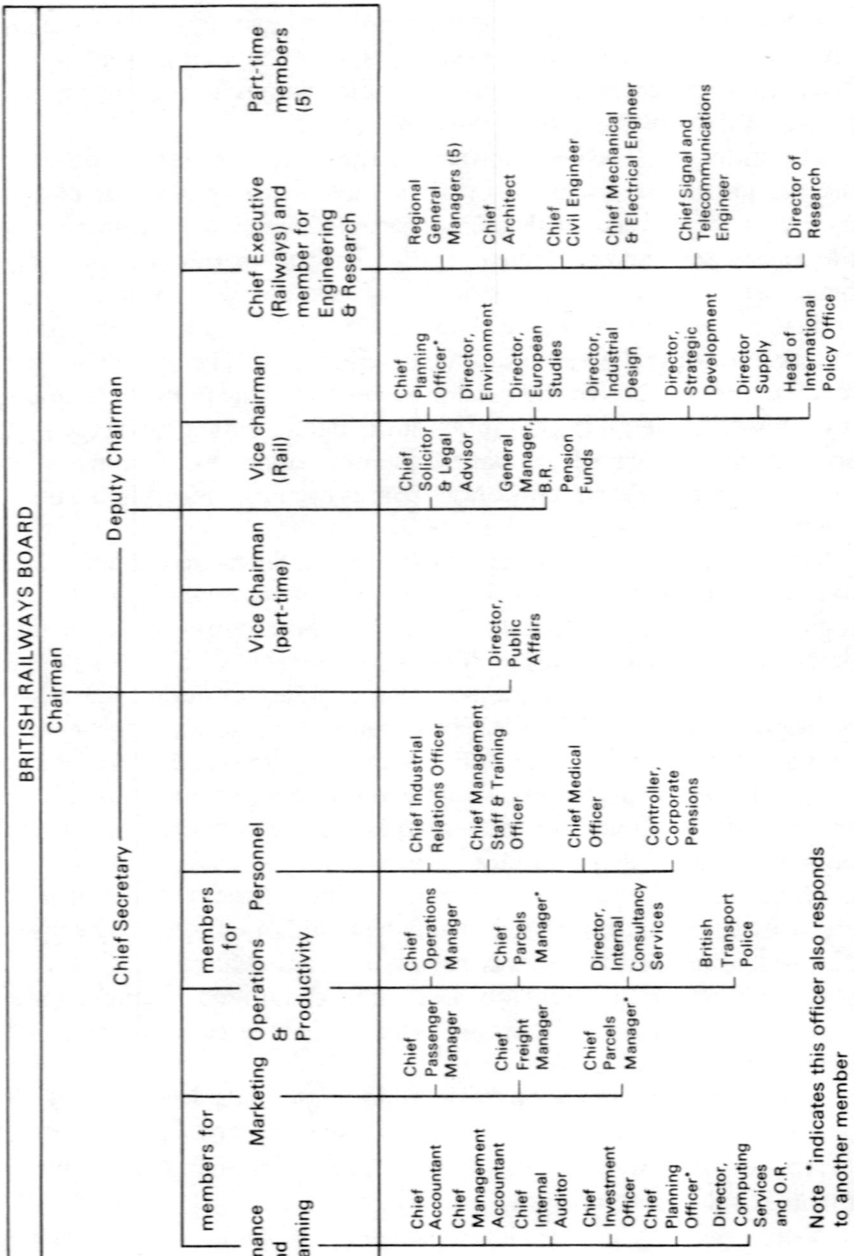

BRITISH RAILWAYS BOARD

Chairman — Deputy Chairman

Chief Secretary

members for Finance and Planning | Marketing | Operations & Productivity | members for Personnel | Vice Chairman (part-time) | Vice chairman (Rail) | Chief Executive (Railways) and member for Engineering & Research | Part-time members (5)

members for Finance and Planning
- Chief Accountant
- Chief Management Accountant
- Chief Internal Auditor
- Chief Investment Officer
- Chief Planning Officer*
- Director, Computing Services and O.R.

Marketing
- Chief Passenger Manager
- Chief Freight Manager
- Chief Parcels Manager*

Operations & Productivity
- Chief Operations Manager
- Chief Parcels Manager*
- Director, Internal Consultancy Services
- British Transport Police

members for Personnel
- Chief Industrial Relations Officer
- Chief Management Staff & Training Officer
- Chief Medical Officer
- Controller, Corporate Pensions

Vice Chairman (part-time)
- Director, Public Affairs

Vice chairman (Rail)
- Chief Solicitor & Legal Advisor
- General Manager, B.R. Pension Funds
- Chief Planning Officer*
- Director, Environment
- Director, European Studies
- Director, Industrial Design
- Director, Strategic Development
- Director Supply
- Head of International Policy Office

Chief Executive (Railways) and member for Engineering & Research
- Regional General Managers (5)
- Chief Architect
- Chief Civil Engineer
- Chief Mechanical & Electrical Engineer
- Chief Signal and Telecommunications Engineer
- Director of Research

Note: *indicates this officer also responds to another member

Fig. 4.3 British Railways: board members and main departments

4.1 Railways

This is far and away the biggest business and consists of a national railway network providing passenger, freight and parcels services. In terms of turnover, it represents about 85% of the total business. It is divided into five regions, which are in turn divided into divisions and areas. Each region is headed by a general manager whose status can be compared with that of a managing director of one of the other businesses. The regional and divisional organisations are functionally constructed, broadly covering marketing (passenger and freight and parcels separately), operations (running of trains and terminals), mechanical and electrical engineering (maintenance of rolling stock and plant), civil engineering (maintenance of permanent way and structures), signal and telecommunication engineering (maintenance of trackside signalling and telecommunications equipment), accounting (financial accounting and management information systems), personnel (industrial relations and general staff matters) and planning (which, in this context, is about investment programming and monitoring). The divisions and areas are of three types: traffic, civil engineering and signal and telecommunications engineering.

The area managers are responsible to the divisional operating managers, mechanical and electrical engineers, civil engineers and signal and telecommunications engineers, respectively. The traffic divisions have at their head offices managers covering marketing, operations, mechanical and electrical engineering, accounting and personnel. This is not the case for the civil or signalling and telecommunications engineering divisions which obtain their personnel input from the traffic side personnel manager and their finance and planning inputs from the regional level. The Scottish Region is untypical, however, in that it does not have traffic divisions and the traffic area managers respond direct to the regional operating or mechanical and electrical engineering managers. Further, on the Southern Region, the finance and planning activities are centralised at regional level.

An attempt was made to standardise the organisation by eliminating the divisional level following a consultant's report[1] but this was abandoned in 1975 because of union and staff opposition and the likely high costs involved in staff movement and general dislocation of administration if the recommendations were followed.

The Railways business covers three sub-businesses which are the passenger business, the freight business and the parcels business. To a large extent, these businesses share the same resources from track to locomotives to administrative manpower. One of the best indicators of the size of the Railways business is the size of the network lines. At the end of 1978 there were 11 123 route miles of track, of which 74% (8247 route miles) was for joint passenger/freight and parcels traffic use and almost 20% (2178 route miles) for freight only. The track mileage of running lines is approximately twice (22 138) the route mileage, being made up largely of two-track lines, with some single and some greater than two-track facilities, notably in the commuter areas.

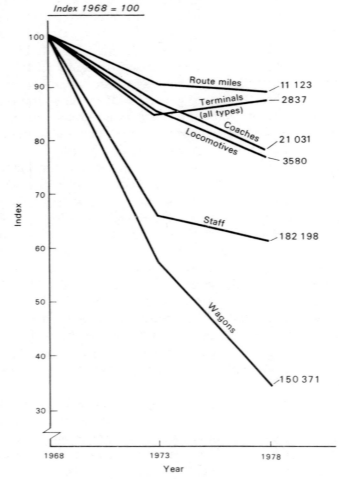

Fig. 4.4 Railway resources: 1968, 1973 and 1978

The resources used in conjunction with this network are considerable. For example, at the end of 1978 there were 2364 passenger stations, 15 parcels depots and 458 freight depots, making 2837 terminals in all. There were 3580 locomotives, 21 031 coaches (16 601 passenger) and 150 371 railway owned freight vehicles. The number of staff was 182 198, including corporate and common services staff. The trend of some of these resources is given in fig. 4.4.

The passenger business is the largest although it has become so largely because of the decline of freight. Recent business volume data in respect of this business alone are given in fig. 4.5.

Index 1973 = 100

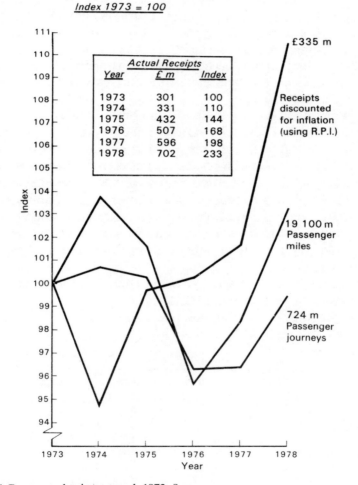

Actual Receipts		
Year	*£ m*	*Index*
1973	301	100
1974	331	110
1975	432	144
1976	507	168
1977	596	198
1978	702	233

£335 m

Receipts discounted for inflation (using R.P.I.)

19 100 m Passenger miles

724 m Passenger journeys

Fig. 4.5 Passenger business trend, 1973–8

It can be seen that since 1973 there has been a significant increase in passenger receipts, after discounting for inflation, using the retail price index. The difference between this receipts line and the trend line of passenger miles (which is the sum of the miles travelled by the individual passengers) is a reasonable indication of the extent of *real price* increases, and this is the sense in which the term is used in the rest of this book. It is interesting to note that the difference was negative in 1974 and to a small extent in 1975. This reflected the effect of low price increases in 1973 and the early part of 1974. Since then the trend of real pricing has been positive.

The volume of business, measured in terms of passenger miles (a more useful measure than passenger journeys) fell during 1975 and 1976 when there were substantial real price increases. Since 1976 business volume has risen because price increases have been closer to the rate of inflation and because of investment-based growth in the main-line services. Further details of the effect of price increases are given in chapters 5 and 7.

For planning purposes, the passenger business is divided into four sectors. These are Inter-city, London and South East (L. & S.E.) Passenger Transport Executives (P.T.E.) and Other Provincial. The Inter-city sector covers express trains between major towns and the London and South East sectors covers the London commuter area. The Passenger Transport Executives' sector covers the commuter services wholly or mostly within the boundaries of the six metropolitan counties in England and the one in Scotland (Strathclyde). The remaining 'green field' services are grouped together and known as the Other Provincial sector.

Between 1975 and 1978 the passenger miles (in thousand million) were distributed as shown in table 4.1.

The reduction of 1100 million passenger miles in 1976 compared

Table 4.1

	1975	1976	1977	1978
Inter-city	8.8	8.0	8.4	9.0
L. & S.E.	7.3	7.1	7.3	7.6
P.T.E.s	1.6	1.6	1.5	1.5
Other Provincial	1.1	1.0	1.0	1.0
	18.8	17.7	18.2	19.1

with 1975 was not evenly spread, with 800 million having arisen in the Inter-city sector, compared with 200 million in the L. & S.E. sector. This represents the greater ability to resist price increases in the Inter-city sector by reduced travel or travel by alternative mode. This is less likely in the commuter areas, particularly London and South East which, whilst not being captive markets, have a marked tendency in that direction. The continuation of the general economic slump was not considered to be a major cause of the decline in 1976. Measured in terms of consumer expenditure, the slump was greater in 1975. The rise in prices produced a real growth in receipts in 1976 over 1975 (i.e. a rate in excess of inflation as measured by the R.P.I.). The reduction in passenger miles and journeys in 1976 was considered to be due largely to the resistance to the extent of the price increases.

The freight business is the second largest and its recent receipts and volume data are given in fig. 4.6 covering the years from 1973 to 1977.

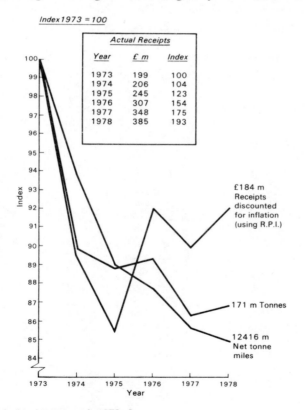

Actual Receipts		
Year	£ m	Index
1973	199	100
1974	206	104
1975	245	123
1976	307	154
1977	348	175
1978	385	193

Index 1973 = 100

£184 m Receipts discounted for inflation (using R.P.I.)

171 m Tonnes

12416 m Net tonne miles

Fig. 4.6 Freight business trend, 1973–8

It can be seen from fig. 4.6 that discounted receipts have increased since 1975 despite volume of carryings falling substantially. The losses of traffic have reflected the state of the economy, in the main, rather than the extent of price increases, and a change of mix.

For planning and control purposes, the freight business carryings are divided into fourteen commodities within two sectors: Train Load and Less than Train Load. For many years, the Less than Train Load sector has been in decline, with a partial transfer to the Train Load sector. This has largely been in response to changing demand but also reflect the B.R.B.'s attitude to the relatively poor economics of the Less than Train Load sector which has an inefficient resource utilisation record. This matter is considered in strategic terms in chapter 9.

A broad analysis of the distribution of the 1978 freight carryings is given in fig. 4.7. The Train Load sector relates to the movement of complete train loads of traffic between two points, usually without intermediate marshalling. The Less Than Train Load sector traffic requires this intermediate marshalling and covers all commodities. Almost all

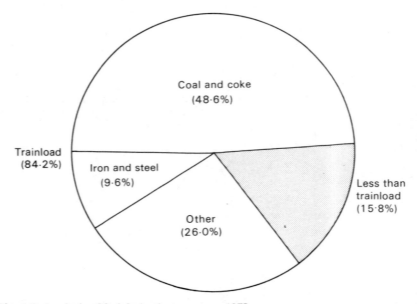

Fig. 4.7 Analysis of freight business tonnes, 1978

of the Train Load traffic is subject to negotiated contract rates, many of which have price variation clauses which tie price increases to movements in national price indices such as the Retail Prices Index and the Wholesale Prices Index. Approximately 25% of the 1978 tonnes was carried in wagons owned by customers and there is a marked trend towards this type of transit, which requires a long-term commitment. Negotiated rates also apply in the Less Than Train Load sector but here scale rates are frequently used because much of the traffic is *ad hoc* in nature.

Parcels is the smallest of the businesses and is split about one-third/two-thirds between traffic which is collected and/or delivered by road (by National Carriers Limited, a subsidiary of the National Freight Corporation, as agents of British Rail) and that which is brought to the station or parcels depot by the customer and also collected at the destination terminal. Traffic in this latter category includes newspapers and post office letter mail and parcels. The distribution of the receipts during 1978 is described in fig. 4.8.

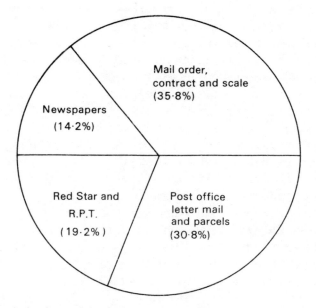

Fig. 4.8 Analysis of parcels business turnover, 1978

The 'Red Star' parcels (parcels carried at premium rates on nominated passenger trains), registered parcels (R.P.T.) and post office letter mail are carried in passenger trains. Newspapers are carried partly in passenger trains and partly in special newspaper trains. The collected and/or delivered traffic (Agreed Flat Rate), scale traffic and parcels post is carried in parcels trains. The bulk of the traffic is conveyed under negotiated rates, the exceptions being Scale, Red Star and R.P.T.

Each of the three Railways businesses is important in its own right but not necessarily to the same extent. The overall Railways business is thus a complex mixture of a number of quite different sub-businesses which are, in some cases, important in providing a vital national service and, in other cases, of secondary importance. The strategic development of the Railways must recognise these factors, incorporating its strengths and allowing for its weaknesses.

4.2 British Rail Engineering Limited (B.R.E.L.)

This is a mechanical and electrical engineering company providing a rolling stock maintenance facility to the Railways activity in respect of major repairs and the supply of materials for day-to-day maintenance at Railways depots. This company also manufactures most of the rolling stock for British Rail. However, B.R.E.L. also trades with third parties in both the maintenance and manufacturing fields, but this is a minor part of the business transacted. The repair and manufacturing facilities are located at installations known as 'main works', of which there are thirteen with a total staff of 35 647 at the end of 1978. This makes B.R.E.L. one of the largest engineering concerns in the United Kingdom. Part of the rolling stock marketing facility is undertaken by B.R.E.–Metro Limited, which is a joint company owned by B.R.E.L. and Metro Cammell Laird Limited, who manufacture urban rapid transit vehicles.

The size of the rolling stock maintenance and building programme was such that the British Railways Board transferred the major depots to this separate company in 1969. Part of the purpose of this was to enable the company to develop its distinctive competence to undertake work for third party companies and to facilitate the manufacture of rolling stock for export. Prior to January 1970 the Railway workshops were specifically prohibited from competing with the private sector for the construction of rolling stock in the United Kingdom or for export.

The size of this company is best judged by considering its turnover which was £313.6 m in 1978 of which £29.2 m did not relate to the Railways business. This level of external trading is obviously quite small and although orders worth £50 m were received in 1978, which was a record level, B.R.E.L. is making only a minor impact (with major railway developments in third world countries) in the vast amount of international trade in this field. However, the main function of B.R.E.L. is to provide an efficient and economic service to the Railways business, the external trading being a bonus. Of the staff numbers employed by B.R.E.L. at the end of 1978, 24 000 were estimated to be engaged on maintenance work and 9000 on construction work for the Railways business.

4.3 British Transport Hotels Limited (B.T.H.)

This is a hotel and catering company, owning hotels in main centres and providing railway station catering and catering on board trains. It is one of the largest hotel and catering companies in the United Kingdom. At the end of 1978 it owned 29 hotels and provided catering units of varying sizes at 234 railway stations. In addition B.T.H. provide restaurant and/or buffet services on most of the Inter-city trains. Volume of turnover amounted to £83.5 m in 1978. This was made up of train catering–£16.6 m, station catering–£33.2 m and hotels–£33.7 m.

The station and train catering is undertaken on an agency basis for the Railways and the resulting profit or loss is brought to account as part of the Railways trading account. The profit or loss on hotel trading is retained within B.T.H. accounts. This difference in treatment recognises the fact that the B.R.B. regards the station and train catering activities as part of the rail passenger transport package. Thus, the Railways business management is in the initiative in much of the decision-making, with B.T.H. acting as agent for provision of the service. The staff numbers employed by British Transport Hotels at the end of 1978 were 10 783.

4.4 British Railways Property Board

This is a property company administering the letting of sites and buildings within areas being used by British Rail (known as operational property) and the letting and sale of sites and buildings not being used (non-operational). The 'Property Board' as it is called is among the five largest property owners in the United Kingdom and undertakes many large development projects, usually near the stations of large towns and often with private developers. Turnover in 1978 amounted to £34.2 m; this consisted of operational property, £22.5 m and non-operational property, £11.7 m. At 31 December 1978, the Property Board portfolio consisted of 140 000 individual properties, licences, easements and wayleaves.

The letting of operational property is regarded as another adjunct of Railways and the profit thereon is credited to the Railways trading account. The profit on the non-operational account is retained within the accounts of the B.R. Property Board. This profit results from the letting of property declared non-operational and the development and sale of sites, all of which would have been declared non-operational sometime beforehand. The capital value of the non-operational property holding was assessed in 1978 at £183 m. When property is declared non-operational its assessed value is credited to the Railways cash flow account and thus the Property Board capital profits represent profits in excess of these transfer values. Much of the effort of the Property Board is directed towards the development of sites in association with other organisations. The number of staff employed by the B.R. Property Board at the end of 1978 was 1099.

4.5 Sealink U.K. Ltd

This is a shipping company formed on 1 January 1979 which was previously known as the Shipping and International Services Division. It provides passenger and freight services to Northern Ireland, Eire, parts of the Continent and some offshore islands, including the Channel Islands and the Isle of Wight. In company with the French Railways, Zeeland Steamship Company and Belgian Marine Transport Authority, the Company operates services under the brand name of 'Sealink' carrying passengers and cars on ten routes to Europe. Together they represent the largest shipping fleet of its kind in Europe, operating seventy-four vessels on twenty-eight routes.

Sealink U.K. Ltd owned thirty-nine ships on 1 January 1979, jointly owned three and leased fourteen. The recent carryings and turnover figures are given in fig. 4.9. Again the receipts are discounted for inflation using the retail prices index.

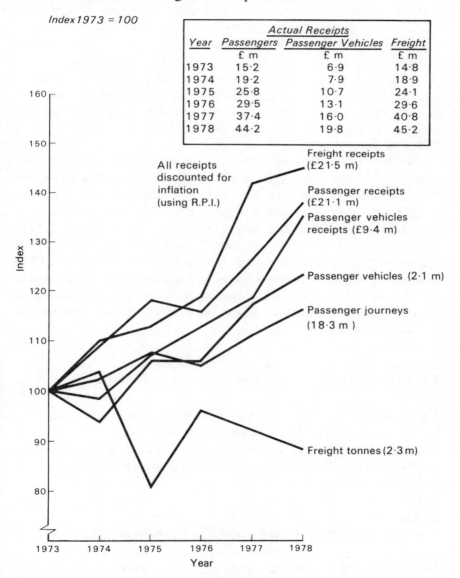

Index 1973 = 100

| Year | Actual Receipts | | |
	Passengers	Passenger Vehicles	Freight
	£ m	£ m	£ m
1973	15·2	6·9	14·8
1974	19·2	7·9	18·9
1975	25·8	10·7	24·1
1976	29·5	13·1	29·6
1977	37·4	16·0	40·8
1978	44·2	19·8	45·2

All receipts discounted for inflation (using R.P.I.)

Freight receipts (£21·5 m)

Passenger receipts (£21·1 m)

Passenger vehicles receipts (£9·4 m)

Passenger vehicles (2·1 m)

Passenger journeys (18·3 m)

Freight tonnes (2·3 m)

Fig. 4.9 Sealink U.K.–business trend, 1973–8

This is a highly competitive business, with a number of efficient and successful private operators in the field. Trading is made more difficult by the extent of the summer peaking on passenger ships. The growth in passenger and passenger vehicles receipts since 1976 is slightly greater than would be expected from volume growth and results from real price increases. As far as freight receipts are concerned, the fall in tonnage has been more than offset by real price increases.

Associated with Sealink U.K. Ltd is the harbours account which is maintained separately although run mainly by the company. This is done to establish the economics of the harbours activity which is credited with harbour dues and fees for handling services. The 1978 receipts of this harbours account amounted to £17.6 m. Staff employed by Sealink U.K. Ltd, including harbour staff, numbered 10 565 at the end of 1978.

The company divides the services into four sectors for planning and control. The first covers those services considered to have an on-going viable future. The second covers those which have a vital railway requirement for their continuation which will be the subject of a contractual arrangement. The third covers those services which are loss-making and the fourth the statutory services.

It is a wholly owned subsidiary of the B.R.B. financed by one-third equity capital and two-thirds loan capital. The intention, following the new limited company status, is to accelerate investment and come to terms with the railway business about support payments for the services in sector 2.

4.6 British Railways Hovercraft Company Limited

This company was one of the first in the field in the United Kingdom. It is a relatively small organisation operating just two hovercraft to France. The 1978 turnover was £5.6 m mainly resulting from 608 000 passenger journeys and 94 000 motor vehicles. Staff employed at the end of 1978 numbered 495.

4.7 Transportation Systems and Market Research Limited

This is a management consultancy company known as 'Transmark' providing assistance to overseas governments and railways on general railway matters. Gross income in 1978 amounted to £4.5 m in connection with work on sixty-nine projects in twenty-nine countries.

4.8 Freightliners Limited

This is a freight transport company providing inland transit of containers by road and by rail. This company was jointly owned by the National Freight Corporation and the B.R.B. who had 51 and 49% respectively. However in August 1978 it reverted to British Rail and is run as a separate wholly owned subsidiary. The 1978 turnover amounted to £51 m.

4.9 British Transport Advertising Limited

This is an advertising company jointly owned with the National Bus Company (N.B.C.) and providing advertising space on B.R.B. sites, N.B.C. sites and N.B.C. buses. The company's rail division achieved a gross income of £5.2 m in 1978 and attributed a net surplus of £2.6 m to the Railways business.

As we have proceeded to examine each of these businesses in turn, it should have become clear that each of them is Railways-related in a trading sense, apart from the organisational connection. It could be argued that each is a logical extension of providing a railway service. The fact that the B.R.B. has not diversified beyond these logical extensions can be explained by the fact that the Acts and other government instruments governing the nationalised industries generally prevent such diversification. The *1962 Transport Act* which created the B.R.B., as amended by other Acts, closely controls any branching-out that the B.R.B. may consider and places the emphasis on activities closely related to the Railways business. Even the Property Board was deemed necessary to cope with the large supply of land and buildings available for sale, letting and development, which resulted from the run-down of the Railways.

FIVE

British Rail–Financial Situation

This chapter follows up the general situation described in chapter 4 by giving a fairly detailed analysis of British Rail's financial history between 1963 and 1978 and its current obligations and prospects. (The figures and tables relate to calendar years unless otherwise stated.)

5.1 Financial history

There can be very few people in Britain who are not aware that 'the railways' have been in a difficult financial state, requiring huge grant payments and all this despite capital reconstructions designed to reduce the depreciation and interest charges to the profit-and-loss account. However, nearly every other large railway in the world makes a loss and their continued existence rests largely on the assumption that they fulfil a social and environmental need. This section is concerned with examining the financial situation of British Rail since 1963, commenting particularly on recent results. In doing this, the non-railway businesses will not be covered in much depth because their profits and losses are small compared with that of the Railways business. Much of the information given here emanates from the B.R.B. annual accounts but with some information not previously published.

When the British Railways Board was established in 1963 the financial situation was already rather desperate because of growing road competition, and it was hoped that the B.R.B. could develop plans to re-shape the Railways' passenger business and develop the

Table 5.1 B.R.B.–consolidated profit-and-loss account (£ m)

	1963	1964	1965	1966	1967	1968
Surplus/(Deficit) of each activity*						
Railways	(81.6)	(67.5)	(73.1)	(71.6)	(90.4)	(83.5)
Ships	4.7	5.1	4.9	3.7	4.7	4.6
Harbours	0.2	0.2	0.1	(0.1)	0.3	0.1
Hotels	0.9	1.2	0.9	0.7	0.8	0.8
Non-operational property	2.3	2.3	2.4	2.2	2.4	2.5
Hovercraft				(0.1)	(0.1)	(0.2)
	(73.5)	(58.7)	(64.8)	(65.2)	(82.3)	(75.7)
Other expenditure	2.4	4.0	6.8	5.4	4.4	4.5
	(75.9)	(62.7)	(71.6)	(70.6)	(86.7)	(80.2)
Other income	0.1	0.2	0.1	0.1	0.2	0.1
	(75.8)	(62.5)	(71.5)	(70.5)	(86.5)	(80.1)
Interest	58.1	58.4	60.9	64.2	66.5	67.3
Surplus/(Deficit)	(133.9)	(120.9)	(132.4)	(134.7)	(153.0)	(147.4)

* This is generally the result of each business, all differences being negligible in this context. The railways activity includes the surplus on the letting of operational property.

Railways' freight train-load sector to eliminate gradually the losses over a period of years. Dr Beeching was appointed chairman and he sponsored the production of a re-shaping report for the railways portion of the business. The emerging financial results are given in table 5.1. It can be seen that the expected results did not occur and, consequently, deficit grants were received from government to cancel the losses and prevent any growth in the interest burden which would have arisen if the deficits had been met by borrowings. A more detailed commentary can be provided by examining the Railway results in more depth. The key figures are given in table 5.2 and, to make them more meaningful, an estimate of the Railways' share of the interest burden has been recorded as a charge to that business. This estimate is quite realistic and is based on cash flow data.

The outline of what occurred is clear. The passenger business receipts increased despite a very considerable reduction in route miles

Table 5.2 Railways--profit-and-loss account (£ m)

	1963	1964	1965	1966	1967	1968
Receipts						
Passenger	161.8	167.2	173.0	179.4	179.7	185.1
Freight/parcels	292.8	291.6	283.9	275.3	250.3	262.4
Miscellaneous	8.5	9.5	9.3	9.1	8.7	9.0
	463.1	468.3	466.2	463.8	438.7	456.5
Working expenses	550.2	541.6	545.7	542.1	536.1	547.1
	(87.1)	(73.3)	(79.5)	(78.3)	(97.4)	(90.6)
Ancillary income	5.6	5.8	6.4	6.7	7.0	7.1
Surplus/(Deficit) (before interest)	(81.5)	(67.5)	(73.1)	(71.6)	(90.4)	(83.5)
Interest (share*)	49.0	49.0	52.0	55.0	57.0	58.0
Surplus/(Deficit) (after interest)	(130.5)	(116.5)	(125.1)	(126.6)	(147.4)	(141.5)

* Assessed share (approx.).

resulting from the 'Beeching' cuts. These route miles in fact dropped from 17 481 at the beginning of 1963 to 12 447 at the end of 1968 causing immense publicity and concern about service withdrawals. On the other hand, the freight/parcels business and, in particular, the freight business suffered considerable receipts losses reflecting a volume reduction of some twenty-eight million tons. Coupled with the receipts situation, the large working expenses reductions associated with the 'Beeching' cuts and other economies were almost completely offset by cost increases (especially pay increases) in the years 1964–8 inclusive. Thus, the deficit situation remained at a high and slightly increasing level despite the extensive action taken and the considerable trauma involved, including a 38% reduction in rail staff to 296 274.

The realisation that the Railway deficits would not be reduced led, in part, to the introduction of the *Transport Act 1968* which covered the following main issues, all of which took effect from 1 January 1969.

(a) A large capital reconstruction designed to reduce depreciation and interest charges. This involved writing down the value of assets and the value of government borrowings.

(b) The calculation of, and grant aid for, the deficits on passenger services determined to be socially necessary. These grants to be paid by government and the newly created Passenger Transport Executives, as appropriate.

(c) The elimination of general deficit financing.

(d) The transfer of the loss-making sundries portion of the rail freight business to the newly formed National Freight Corporation. The sundries business was the 'large parcels' sector (56 lb to 3 tons per consignment) which usually involved collection and delivery by road vehicle.

(e) The creation of B.R.E.L.

(f) The creation of Freightliners Limited to take over and develop the small freightliner activity started in 1966.

The idea was that these changes would at least produce a profitable Railways business which when coupled with the fairly healthy non-railway businesses would mean a profitable B.R.B. What happened in the event can be seen in table 5.3 which covers the years from 1969 to 1974 inclusive.

The 1968 Act required the B.R.B. to break even on profit-and-loss account one year with another after receipt of the passenger grants. In 1969, 1970 and 1971 this was achieved and the Act seemed to be a big success. From 1972 onwards, however, things went badly awry, particularly in the Railways business, as can be seen in table 5.4.

In 1971 total receipts excluding grant aid increased by £22 m. It was estimated that this resulted from an increase of £55 m from price increases (pricing action), offset by an estimated decline of £33 m due to a reduction in the volume of freight traffic carried (volume of receipts). Working expenses increased by £46 m as a result of cost increases of £59 m (mostly pay awards), partly offset by improvements in the volume of expenses of £13 m due to economies. The grant showed a slight increase only.

There was worse to come in 1972, when total receipts increased by only £5 m excluding grant aid. This resulted from an estimated increase of £36 m because of pricing action, offset by an estimated decline of £31 m due to a decrease in the volume of receipts. Working expenses increased by £40 m as a result of cost increases of £59 m (mostly pay awards), again partly offset by improvements of £19 m

Table 5.3   B.R.B–consolidated profit-and-loss account (£ m)

	1969	1970	1971	1972	1973	1974
Surplus/(Deficit) of each activity*						
Railways	48.5	47.4	26.2	17.8	(5.1)	(96.9)
Ships	4.5	3.2	2.0	3.3	2.6	(1.8)
Harbours	0.3	(0.1)	(0.5)	0.1	0.2	—
Hotels	0.9	1.2	1.2	1.4	1.2	0.7
Non-operational property	2.7	3.1	4.1	4.9	5.5	5.3
Hovercraft	(0.3)	(0.4)	(0.3)	(0.2)	0.1	(0.5)
B.R.E.L.	0.1	0.1	0.2	0.4	0.4	0.6
Freightliners (share)	(1.1)	(0.4)	—	(0.2)	0.5	—
	55.6	54.1	32.9	27.5	5.4	(92.6)
Ancillary income	0.6	0.4	0.5	0.6	3.9	10.2
Corporate expenses	—	2.8	3.2	3.2	3.6	3.5
Surplus/(Deficit) (before interest)	56.2	51.7	30.2	24.9	5.7	(85.9)
Interest	41.5	42.2	45.6	51.1	57.3	71.9
Surplus/(Deficit) (after interest)	14.7	9.5	(15.4)	(26.2)	(51.6)	(157.8)
Grant aid included in Railways figures	61.2	61.7	63.1	68.2	91.4	154.3

* This is generally the result of each business, all differences being negligible, in this context.
The railways activity includes the surplus on the letting of operational property.

due to economies in the volume of expenses. There was one bright,
though temporary, feature: this was the receipt of a special grant for
holding down prices at the request of government. This amounted to
£27 m and explains the large increase under Receipts–miscellaneous.
The grant aid increased by £5 m, mainly reflecting the cost increases.
The total interest burden was now beginning to rise sharply and the
railway share in particular. This reflected the fact that the new stream
of deficits had to be borrowed from government as well as the usual
borrowings to finance investment in excess of depreciation provisions.

   In 1973 the railway loss, after charging a share of interest burden,
amounted to £56 m compared with £28 m in 1972 and £12 m in 1971. In

Table 5.4   Railway–profit-and-loss account (£ m)

	1969	1970	1971	1972	1973	1974
Receipts						
Passenger–fares	205.4	227.8	261.0	274.1	297.3	328.8
–grant aid	61.2	61.7	63.1	68.2	91.4	154.3
Freight	195.5	208.2	193.9	183.3	198.5	205.5
Parcels	60.0	62.4	65.0	68.6	73.8	75.3
Miscellaneous	10.6	11.4	12.2	38.2	12.1	11.9
	532.7	571.5	595.2	632.4	673.1	775.8
Working expenses	491.6	532.0	578.0	625.1	688.6	882.8
	41.1	39.5	17.2	7.3	(15.5)	(107.0)
Ancillary income	7.5	7.9	9.0	10.5	10.4	10.1
Surplus/(Deficit) (before interest)	48.6	47.4	26.2	17.8	(5.1)	(96.9)
Interest (share*)	36.0	36.0	38.0	46.0	51.0	65.0
Surplus/(Deficit) (after interest)	12.6	11.4	(11.8)	(28.2)	(56.1)	(161.9)

* Assessed share (approx.).

fact the 1973 results were in many ways comparable with the 1972 figures because the 1972 loss would have been £55 m without the 'once-off' pricing grant of £27 m. Pricing action produced £26 m in 1973 which was hopelessly inadequate to deal with cost increases of £51 m. However, receipts volume improved by £18 m but this was largely offset by a working expenses volume increase of £13 m. Much of the overall deterioration was covered by the grant aid which increased by £23 m, so the net situation basically boiled down to the value of the non-receipt of the pricing grant for a second year.

The year 1974 was worse and might be described as a 'watershed'. The loss, after interest, increased from £52 m to £158 m for the B.R.B. and from £56 m to £162 m for the Railways business. Receipts pricing action in the Railways business produced £56 m in 1974 which bore no comparison with the cost increase of £184 m. These cost increases reflected the general level of inflation (including oil prices) but mainly consisted of pay awards including a September 'comparability' award. This was coupled with further receipts volume losses of £16 m and working expenses volume increases of £10 m. With an industrial recession under way, the receipts losses were on the freight and parcels side, with the passenger business improving by £5 m. Industrial disputes and the three-day week caused a drop of £14 m and the remaining £7 m reflected the general economic recession. The grant aid increased from £91 m to £154 m, but with the remaining Railway deficit being £162 m and the overall deficit being £158 m, both figures allowing for a further increase in the interest burden, it was necessary for further government action to be contemplated.

The first action was the receipt of a special grant of £215 m to meet the B.R.B. cash shortfall. Of this £157.8 m was applied to write off the loss for 1974. Hence, there was the end of the constraint of no deficit financing. The second action was the enacting of the *Railways Act 1974* which created a new set of rules. The main elements were:

(a) The establishment of a public service obligation (P.S.O.) which enabled the government to give grant aid to the passenger business as a whole (on top of that already provided by the Passenger Transport Executives).

(b) The requirements that the freight and parcels businesses as combined should cover their direct working expenses and their share of joint expenses (infrastructure and administration) calculated on an avoidable basis. This avoidable cost calculation was based on the assumption that the railway exists primarily for the passenger business.

(c) A further capital reconstruction and shorter depreciation lives for wagons, coupled with the reclassification of most infrastructure investment as 'revenue investment' (to be charged therefore to working expenses) rather than capital investment, as hitherto. This last item was seen as a step towards inflation accounting.

(d) Provision for grants to freight customers to assist with the establishment of new private sidings.

(e) Grant aid arrangements in respect of pension fund deficiencies.

The Act came into operation on 1 January 1975 and the accounts from 1975 to 1978 showed results as depicted in table 5.5.

It can be seen that one of the rules was 'broken' immediately, in that the government provided a freight grant which came out of their contingency fund. The P.S.O. grant contained in the Railways figures amounted to £321.8 m (and arrears of grant aid under the 1968 Act

Table 5.5   B.R.B.–consolidated profit-and-loss account (£ m)

	1975	1976	1977	1978
Surplus/(Deficit) of each activity*				
Railways	(42.3)	0.1	44.8	37.8
Ships	(5.2)	(2.2)	6.5	9.1
Harbours	(0.4)	1.0	2.7	3.1
Hotels	0.8	0.7	1.5	1.0
Non-operational property	5.5	6.3	7.0	7.0
Hovercraft	(0.2)	—	(0.6)	(2.2)
B.R.E.L.	0.5	0.4	0.6	0.1
Freightliners (share)	(0.8)	0.3	0.3	0.8
	(42.1)	6.6	62.8	56.7
Ancillary income	17.9	10.8	9.7	7.4
Corporate expenses	4.1	3.7	4.1	5.8
Surplus/(Deficit) (before interest)	(28.3)	13.7	68.4	58.3
Interest and exchange losses/(gains)	32.5	43.4	38.5	51.6
Taxation	—	0.2	0.2	0.2
Surplus/(Deficit) (after interest)	(60.8)	(29.9)	29.7	6.5
Special grant for non-passenger deficit	66.3	35.2	5.5	—
Grant adjustments	—	—	(8.2)	(0.1)
Adjusted surplus/(deficit) (after interest)	5.5	5.3	27.0	6.4

* This is generally the result for each business, all differences being negligible in this context. The railways activity includes the surplus on the letting of operational property.

were £3.3 m) in 1975, £319.1 m in 1976, £363.5 m in 1977 and £434.1 m in 1978. The Railways content of these figures is given in table 5.6.

The difference between the freight deficit grant and the surplus/(deficit) before interest consisted mainly of the interest charge for the Railways business (the P.S.O. grant includes interest) and a charge for corporate expenses. However, it also included any difference between the P.S.O. grant received from government under the grant

Corporate Management and Financial Planning

Table 5.6   Railway–profit-and-loss account (£ m)

	1975	1976	1977	1978
Receipts				
Passenger–fares	428.9	505.1	593.4	701.8
–grants (P.S.O. including P.T.E.)	324.1	319.1	363.5	434.1
Freight	244.8	307.0	348.2	384.4
Parcels	87.7	98.2	109.6	119.4
Miscellaneous	12.8	14.4	15.7	18.0
	1098.3	1243.8	1430.4	1657.7
Working expenses	1150.9	1255.8	1399.6	1634.6
	(52.6)	(12.0)	30.8	23.1
Ancillary income	10.3	12.1	13.9	14.7
Surplus/(Deficit) before interest	(42.3)	0.1	44.7	37.8
Special grant for freight deficit	66.3	35.2	(2.7)	—

rules and the final passenger loss for the year. The differences were relatively small in 1975, 1976 and 1978 but amounted to a profit of approximately £22 m in 1977.

In 1975 receipts from pricing action produced £170 m, which did not match the cost increases of £222 m. This was not because of the percentages applied but because the working expenses were so far in excess of receipts (excluding grants) that equivalent percentages produced an ever-widening gap. In real terms the net profit situation improved slightly. The receipts volume variance was an adverse change of £17 m which was partly offset by an improvement of £3 m in the volume of working expenses. The change in receipts lay in the freight and parcels businesses in the main, again reflecting the continued economic recession. A further £49 m increase in working expenses was caused by the changes in the capital accounting rules, whereby investment classed as 'revenue' was charged to working expenses, more than offsetting the reduction in depreciation charges.

In 1976 receipts from pricing action produced £159 m (passenger £75 m, freight £67 m and parcels £17 m) and a further largely uninformed passenger public outcry. However, the pricing/cost increases gap was not widened because of the national pay policy stage 1 which restricted the spring 1976 pay award to £6 per week per employee. Consequently, cost increases were held down to £163 m. Receipts volume variances amounted to a reduction of £9 m, with costs reducing in volume terms by £58 m. This reduction included £24 m revenue investment (i.e. mostly track and signalling) which was temporary in nature.

It can be seen that the 1976 result was considerably better than that for 1975 in real terms. The main reason for the improvement in 1976 was the national pay policy which restricted pay awards well below the general level of inflation.

In 1977 receipts from pricing action produced £132 m (passenger £62 m, freight £51 m and parcels £19 m) and even more public outcry concerning the passenger increases, in view of pay policy. Pay and other cost increases amounted to £128 m, reflecting a much lower percentage increase than applied on the receipts side. The 1977 pay award was restricted to a maximum of £4 per week per employee in line with the national pay policy stage 2. Receipts volume variances amounted to an improvement of £10 m with a £26 m improvement in the passenger side having been offset by reductions of £9 m and £7 m in freight and parcels, respectively. The volume of working expenses increased by £16 m but this figure included an increase in revenue investment of £19 m and £4 m additional depreciation.

In 1978 receipts from pricing action produced £133 m (passenger £74 m, freight £45 m and parcels £14 m). Pay and other cost increases amounted to £148 m, benefiting from the low residual effect of the 1977 pay award. Thus the combined effect of pricing and cost changes was favourable considering that costs were well in excess of receipts. The volume of receipts increased by £19 m with an improvement of £35 m in passenger receipts having been reduced by reductions on the freight and parcels side of £12 m and £4 m, respectively. The volume of working expenses increased by £37 m, mainly in respect of increased revenue investment and engineering maintenance. Additionally, a further £50 m supplementary depreciation (described as a 'passenger rolling stock replacement allowance') was included in the working expenses and included in the P.S.O. grant. This is discussed further in section 5.2.

An appreciation of the current financial position and the achievements from 1976 to 1978 appears in section 5.2. Before moving to that section, however, it is necessary to examine one further element of the B.R.B.'s financial situation. This element is pensions funding which was another major problem dealt with under the *Railways Act 1974*.

Basically, the problem refers to the solvency of the overall pension funds, following the rapid rundown of the number of employees, the methods of investing the funds internally and the severe effect of inflation. There are sixty-five pension schemes and societies, most of which are contributory, that provide pension benefits for B.R. staff. Most current employees (over 85%) are members of one of three large schemes formed in recent years by transferring the bulk of the members from the other schemes. In common with most pension schemes the funds of the three 'modern' schemes are not invested internally but in gilts, equities, property, works of art, etc. The transfer arrangements were not supported by the appropriate levels of funding. Consequently, the board has had to guarantee the so-called 'inherited obligations', although it does not guarantee the benefits accruing from current membership of the 'modern' schemes.

The *1974 Railways Act* provided that the B.R.B. should fund the inherited obligations to be reimbursed by the Secretary of State of the Department of Transport in respect of principal and interest. The B.R.B. is to commence payment of the actuarially assessed debt by eight unequal instalments commencing in 1979 and be reimbursed by the Secretary of State. Interest has been paid since 1 January 1975.

The final amount of the debts under the *Railways Act 1974* will be assessed in 1979. However, six 'funding orders' are already in existence for the total sum of £972.9 m with a minimum level of acknowledged debt of £679.6 m. The 1978 interest payment received by the B.R.B. and passed to the pension funds was £79.3 m.

A further related issue is the outstandings on the investments the old pension funds were making within the British Railways Board on a deposit account basis up to 1973. Following the cessation of this practice, it was decided to repay the pension schemes concerned by five annual instalments, the first of which was paid on 2 January 1974. The *Railways Act 1974* provided for government reimbursement in this case also, and all payments plus interest have now been made.

The actuarial deficiency situation has been recognised for many years but has only become an acute problem during the last decade. Under the B.R.B. financial reconstruction as at 1 January 1969, the then provision was re-assessed on the basis that with interest at 5% credited each year, on the balance carried forward, it would be adequate to meet the board's liabilities when they fell due. By 31

December 1973 the B.R.B. had established that this was not so and an estimated deficiency of £280 m was assessed at that date. As we have noted, even that massive figure has proved inadequate.

5.2 Current obligations and immediate prospects

It may be seen from the key figures shown in table 5.7 that the financial obligations of the B.R.B. to government from 1975 to 1978 were extensive, even excluding borrowings. This burden to the

Table 5.7   Summary of main grants (£ m)

	1975	1976	1977	1978
P.S.O (including P.T.E. grants)	321	319	364	436
P.S.O. adjustment (previous years)	3	5	—	(2)
Non-passenger deficit	66	35	(3)	—
Level crossings	9	10	10	11
Repayment of pensions deposits	35	35	35	34
Interest on pensions deposits	14	8	5	—
Pension deficiency interest	49	65	67	79
Infrastructure (section 56 of *Transport Act 1968*)	8	8	12	1
Research	2	2	2	2
	507	487	492	561

Exchequer has become an emotive subject centred on the fact that the P.S.O. grant amounts to almost half the receipts from passenger customers. There has been a feeling that the situation has been allowed to get out of hand and that financial support of this order is intolerable.

It is generally accepted that the level of grants paid in recent years could not have been avoided if the Railways were to exist in anything like their current size. To some extent, it can be argued that pricing action could have been a bit more severe and some of the cost cutting a little more rigorous, but this would only have made a marginal difference. It is interesting to note, for example, that the financial support is less than one-quarter of the support provided to the Japanese and German railways and is considerably less than many other countries. There has been no way of preventing the effects of the recession or inflation, even in respect of the pay awards. It would be naive to consider that British Rail could have granted its staff pay increases much below the 'going rate' for generally established comparable jobs, no matter what the financial situation.

Whatever the reasonableness of the situation, the government set out in 1975/76 to establish general targets concerning the levels of revenue account grant and investment. The action taken in this respect did not stem particularly from the financial circumstances of British Rail, who were establishing a form of financial targets themselves, but from the size of the national budget deficit which was prompting suggestions that public spending was getting out of control. This gave birth to the 'cash limits' system of control whereby the public sector was allowed to make drawings on the public purse only within a pre-determined level fixed for anything from one to four years. These levels were determined separately for each organisation.

As far as British Rail is concerned, the cash limits procedure has applied since 1976 in respect of the P.S.O. grant, the non-passenger (i.e. freight, parcels and ancillary income) deficit grant and the level of investment. However, as far as investment is concerned there has been an annual 'ceiling' for many years.

In regard to the P.S.O., the basic ground rule is that the level of grant must not exceed the 1975 level in real terms. In practice, this means that the 1975 P.S.O. of £321 m would be allowed to increase to £358 m in 1976, £404 m in 1977 and £490 m in 1978, £544 m in 1979, reflecting the addition of an inflation index and a reduction of £11 m in 1979 (Cmnd 6836, in 1979 price levels). The inflation index in this case is the so called 'G.D.P. deflator' which is the index used to convert expenditure on the Gross Domestic Product to constant prices. Additionally, in 1978, the P.S.O. cash limit was adjusted to take account of the Rolling stock Replacement Allowance of £50 m. This was meant to reduce the capital investment borrowing for the passenger business which in a grant aid situation, has no profits to pay off such funding. Strictly speaking the cash limit procedure applies separately to that part of the P.S.O. which is funded by government and that part which is funded by the P.T.E.s. However, British Rail prefer to regard it as one cash limit.

It can be seen that British Rail was able to work within its P.S.O. cash limit and beat the target by £39 m in 1976, £40 m in 1977 and £56 m in 1978. Thus, in real terms they can be regarded as having improved their P.S.O. financial performance compared with 1975. British Rail have coined the term 'working within the contract' to cover the achievement of the P.S.O. within a pre-determined level which itself is within the cash limit. The permitted level relates to the budget for the year in question as agreed with the Department of Transport before each year commences. In 1976 British Rail beat the contract by £22 m and by £27 m and £6 m in the years 1977 and 1978, respectively.

On the non-passenger side, the cash limit arrangements have been more arbitrary, reflecting the government's intention that there should not be any deficit grant from 1978. The cash limit for 1976 was £60 m and it will be observed that this was beaten by some £25 m. The cash limit for 1977 was originally fixed at £30 m but later reduced to £25 m. Here again the target was well beaten.

On the investment side, the cash limit, or ceiling as it is called, again relates to the achievement of the 1975 level in real terms for 1976 and 1977. However, in this area, inflation is measured according to the Capital Goods Index and not G.D.P. deflator.

It is interesting to reflect on the results for 1976 and 1977. This was a period of heavy price increases but with cost increases held down because of national pay policy. Consequently, it has not been too difficult to achieve the cash limits. Indeed, if the pay awards had been close to the rate of inflation, the P.S.O. cash limit would not have been achieved and the freight/parcels gap would not have been virtually eliminated. However, we have seen that during 1976 and 1977 there were considerable manpower reductions and improvements in the volume of traffic in some areas, reflecting a general improvement in productivity, which also had an important effect.

The overall financial situation seems to have moved from very poor to relatively healthy from 1974 to 1977. This could be considered to be partly a matter of fact and partly a matter of interpretation. Certainly, the results for 1976 and 1977 can be regarded as pleasing because they are lower in real terms than 1975 and well within the cash limits. As such British Rail has not needed to call upon the total amount of financial assistance allocated to it by government. In addition, the concept of the P.S.O. 'contract' has been accepted in all quarters. In fact it is now widely recognised as an integral part of the short-term planning and control procedures of British Rail. Thus, the phrase 'contract payment' is being applied to the passenger business instead of the term subsidy. This is a healthy step forward; the need for an ongoing P.S.O. grant arrangement is recognised, provided that the cash limit procedure is intelligently applied.

The relatively healthy financial state experienced from 1976 to 1978 however is now showing signs of deterioration. The leeway (known as 'headroom') on the P.S.O. grant cash limit is likely to be as low as £10 m in 1979 and the contract figure may be exceeded by as much as £40 m. The main reason for the decline is the fact that the 1979 pay settlement amounted to about 13%, overall, while passenger price increases in January 1979 were only 9%. The pay settlement was, in fact, much higher than anticipated either by government which had hoped for a figure of around 5–7% (the government target was 5%) and by the board when they fixed the passenger price increase. The non-passenger business is expected to make a small loss of about £3–5 m.

This deterioration in the results does not augur well for 1980 and beyond as there is now no headroom for emerging problems. Indeed, depending on the relationship between the 1980 passenger price increase and the 1980 pay settlement, it is quite likely that British Rail will have great difficulty in staying within the P.S.O. cash limit.

However, the situation is, in fact, much worse than so far portrayed. The reason is that a new cash limit procedure has emerged during the second half of 1979, which is far more onerous than the other arrangements. For many years British Rail, in common with other nationalised industries, has been advising government of its overall cash forecasts on a quarterly basis for one to two years ahead. The figures have not been used in a cash limit sense because of the other arrangements already discussed in this section.

In the new system government will use the cash forecast provided at the end of 1978 for the fiscal year 1979/80 as a strict cash limit. This forecast allowed for:
(a) P.S.O. grant–estimated actual
(b) level crossings grant
(c) pension fund deficiency grant
(d) all borrowings to cover investment, changes in working capital, etc.

This forecast covered the expected requirements for the above items and was less than the aggregate of the sums permitted within the constraints of the cash limits already discussed.

Further, the forecast did not allow for a high enough pay award in 1979 and the government allowance for inflation was under-estimated. Moreover, the situation was made worse by an arbitrary cut of £15 m imposed by government. Consequently, the government's cash limit at £715 m for 1979/80 was £38 m below the board's assessment of the actual requirements. The difference between the new cash limit and the figure which would be arrived at by using an aggregate of the previously established cash limits is even wider.

What will eventually emerge is not yet clear. However, for the present it seems quite likely that these will not be re-negotiated, however illogical they may seem to be. Instead, government may require that the 1979/80 financing cash limit be further improved upon in real terms, in 1980/81.

SIX

Financial Planning in British Rail

This chapter is concerned with examining how the overall theories expounded in chapters 2 and 3 are being put into practice within British Rail. As far as possible, we will attempt to follow the layout of those chapters to facilitate cross-referencing. In doing this, it will again be necessary to refer frequently to the model given in fig. 2.2. It will be remembered that the purpose of such a framework is to attempt to make sense of a highly complex situation, through simplification of the complexity to manageable proportions. Clearly no two organisations are alike and differences will arise in their approach to the processes embodied in the corporate/financial planning theory. This chapter will examine one such approach–that of British Rail–and examine how it has been adapted to meet its perceived needs.

6.1 Corporate planning practice

It is probably true to say that aspects of corporate/financial planning have been practised in British Rail ever since its establishment. However, it was not practised within the kind of framework developed in chapter 2 until 1969. This was when corporate planning started in a structured and official sense in British Rail, a little later than a few large organisations but considerably sooner than most, particularly those in the public sector.[1] Considerable progress has since been made in the application of developments in this field.

This progress has been achieved in a large and complex industry, in an intensely political atmosphere and in an industrial relations environment conditioned by past massive manpower reductions.

Further, the effect of unprecedented inflation and the recent general economic depression created unforeseen difficulties. Moreover, government has often been more concerned with attempting to deal with immediate problems than with planning problems concerning future years with a large time span. In 1970 the results of the first formal corporate planning exercise emerged but before this the B.R.B. had been extensively involved in major planning studies. In 1962/63 the 'Reshaping Report' was produced which gave rise to the so called 'Beeching cuts' in unremunerative passenger services and lines. In 1968 the freight business strategy was re-examined and the emphasis, foreshadowed by the Beeching report, was placed on a heavy concentration on the train-load sector at the expense of a partial rundown in the less than train-load sector.

During the late 1960s, corporate planning was beginning to become fashionable and government departments and nationalised industries were considering its adoption with mixed enthusiasm. The British Railways Board and the then Ministry of Transport decided to take the issue very seriously and they jointly commissioned a firm of consultants to prepare an outline of the nature of the task and the recommended procedures for its use, should corporate planning be adopted. The consultants, Cooper Brothers, produced their report entitled *Corporate Planning in British Railways* in 1967. This was submitted to a Joint Steering Group of the British Railways Board and the Ministry of Transport.[2]

The consultants' report considered a corporate planning system in terms of concepts and organisational implications and provided a useful outline of the procedures which should be followed to prepare a corporate plan. Some of the salient features are covered in the next few pages. Cooper Brothers established in their report a series of 'elements' of corporate planning and identified the relationship between them. They summarised their approach in the form of a model, which is given as fig 6.1. It can be seen that the elements are generally similar to those given in the model in fig. 2.2 with the 'control' function exercised within the centre circle. Cooper Brothers explained that forward planning is an integral part of executive management's responsibilities and they clearly regarded the process as being of overriding importance. Briefly, they regarded strategy formulation as the responsibility of board members and headquarters chief officers and action planning by executive management at headquarters and regional level.

Fig. 6.1 Relationship and cycle of the elements of corporate planning

There are some significant differences compared with our model (fig. 2.2). The 'values' and 'policies' do not appear to be fully covered and this seems to be because it was assumed that 'objectives' are laid down by government as are most 'planning parameters'. The report made it clear that the B.R.B. would generally only find it necessary to determine more detailed objectives for parts of the business within such overall objectives. This is considered to mean sub-objectives which can be similar to 'goals' within our explanation, except that there is no particular mention of their being 'marker-points' indicating the timing of events required to be achieved towards the objectives. Instead, they were regarded as objectives sub-divided for responsible management sectors.

The 'planning parameters' were a restricted view of 'values' and 'policies' in that little emphasis is placed on the need to give full consideration to these matters. Instead, it was generally assumed that there would be sufficient rules and regulations laid down by government statutes and departmental instructions to prevent much freedom of action. This view was held to be paramount in the determination of overall objectives.

As we proceed further through both models the differences become less significant. However, it is noticeable that the Cooper Brothers model does not specifically mention the need for an 'outline plan' between the 'strategy' and the 'action plan' items. This, it seems, is to be subsumed under both of these headings, with the term 'strategy' not having the precise meaning that was outlined in fig. 2.2. Neither does the model seek to identify specifically the financial planning elements of the overall process. However, it is considered that this is covered by mention of the words 'financial position' within the central co-ordinating circle.

Given these comments, it is apparent that the concept of corporate planning outlined by Cooper Brothers represents a clear view of the corporate planning process with a system specially designed to meet the needs of British Rail. It has already been emphasised that, whatever normative model is used as the basis of corporate planning, it will have to be considerably modified to meet the needs of the organisation to which it is applied. In relation to British Rail, for example, one of the modifications thought necessary is related to the placing of the planning department in the organisational structure and its responsibilities. For example, it recommended the creation of a strong corporate planning organisation at B.R.B. headquarters, describing this requirement as a condition of effective corporate planning. The terms they used were important, viz:

'The main responsibility of this organisation is to see that planning is done by executive management; it must clearly have a central role in co-ordinating planning activities wherever carried out and in appraising the plans formulated. Moreover, the corporate planning organisation should be active in stimulating the search for new opportunities and new solutions to existing and future problems.'[3]

It is clear that this requirement matches closely the view of the organisational implications given in chapter 2. The accent is on coordination with the correct amount of direct responsibility being left to executive management.

There can be little doubt that the consultants' report provided British Rail with a good concise explanation of the importance of corporate planning, an analysis of its likely effect on the organisation and how to go about it.

As a consequence of the Cooper Brothers' Report, a team was created in 1968/69 under control of an executive director, planning, a senior position just short of board member status. At that time board members were non-executive and executive responsibility within the Railways business was vested in executive directors who were in control of the various departments, with a chief executive carrying overall responsibility to the board. In 1971, the planning responsibility was taken by the controller of corporate planning, who was also given full executive director status. The controller of corporate planning became responsible for production of the Railways element of the corporate plan (known as the Rail Plan) and the consolidation of the overall corporate plan which required a plan from each other business. He also took responsibility for the development of procedures and methods by which the plans were to be compiled and of planning assumptions for each business plan. The assumptions included such things as predicted rates of inflation (as measured by the retail prices index), output (as measured by, for example, gross domestic product and consumers' expenditure) and real earnings.

No attempt has been made to consider overall strategy, objectives or goals for British Rail as a whole. This follows an important recommendation about procedures and methods related to the aggregation of the plans of each business. Cooper Brothers recommended that the corporate plan would be the aggregation of the plans of each business, with each business plan being almost a corporate plan within itself in terms of being largely self-contained. This situation applies today with little stress being laid on the determination of fully corporate objectives and strategy with respect to the British Railways Board's total business. This is discussed in more depth later. Thus, the corporate plan of British Rail tends to be a consolidated document of the respective plans of the businesses and not the British Railways Board's business taken as an entity.

Cooper Brothers further recommended that the individual business plans and the consolidated plan (referred to as the corporate plan) be produced annually, thus recognising the need to keep the contents up-to-date. This is still the intention, but for various reasons there have been only six formal plans during the last nine years; these were in 1970, 1972, 1974, 1975, 1978 and 1979.

The first plan was described as the First Corporate Plan with the Railway business document described as the First Rail Plan. The process of preparing the First Plan set a pattern for the future. A 'Rail Planning Group' was established which was chaired by the executive director, planning (which post later became controller of corporate planning and more recently chief planning officer) and attended by a small number of his staff and a senior 'planning' representative for each major department. The group met and continues to meet; it discusses planning procedures and assumptions to ensure co-ordinated action and progress. The members from outside the corporate planning department cover finance, investment, passenger, freight, parcels, operating, engineering (mechanical and electrical, civil, signal and telecommunications), personnel and B.R.E.L. They are jointly responsible for the production of Rail Plans.

The plans of the other businesses became the responsibilities of the boards of these businesses. Much of their planning work has taken place in similar fashion to those in Rail, with regular planning meetings at a senior level with the guidance of the board of each business. Generally speaking, the chairman of each business planning committee or his representative will be expected to attend any *ad hoc* corporate planning meetings held to discuss the consolidated plan or any guidelines and assumptions which have been issued to those businesses by the chief planning officer. In this connection, the assumptions have usually been similar to those for the Railways business and have not covered discrete strategic issues or objectives. This is indicative of a partial 'bottom-up' approach to corporate planning, each business being expected to determine its strategy in line with a broad objective such as 'break-even financially'. The layout of each business plan–the bulk of which is in the form of an outline plan–has been fairly straightforward with a heavy emphasis on physical and financial forecasts based on a declared outline strategy. The procedures agreed within the 'planning committees' follow closely the forecasting routine given at the end of the forecasting section of chapter 3. That is the marketing specification, leading to the operating (production) specification, etc. through to the financial evaluation. It is similar in every sense to the outline plan box in fig. 2.2. They have not contained detailed programmed events but instead broader annual forecasts of resources and monies, assuming the detailed events to be programmable.

The plans have generally contained forecasts in detail for five or six years with a snapshot view of a tenth year. The financial content has been in constant prices, i.e. base year prices, the base being the budget for the year in which the plan was prepared. The financial evaluation is completed by a summary of the forecasts in future prices based upon forecast changes in the retail prices index.

The comparison with the corporate planning theory given in fig. 2.2 is extremely interesting and it is worthwhile looking at each box of the model in turn. The remarks made will generally apply equally to each of the six plans so far undertaken at the corporate and business level.

There is little evidence of values being expressly considered or how they have influenced subsequent events. The same applies to 'policies' and it is evident that the Cooper Brothers' analysis of the situation is being followed–implicitly at least. The board seems to have relied on the host of rules and regulations which have arisen over the years and the continuance of custom and practice as a substitute for detailed and detached analysis in these areas. For example, there is no explicitly stated view towards such things as technical innovation, product quality, pay scales, etc. Instead, a stance has been established over the years recognising developments in the field resulting from new ideas or fresh crises from within or without. Great reliance has been placed on sparse official government values or policies emerging as discrete instructions or recommendations to do something or not to do something. This might include issues as varied as temporarily freezing prices or improving productivity through manpower reductions.

It would be difficult to argue, therefore, that the B.R.B. has an agreed set of values and policies in respect of the Railways passenger business. Over the years, a theme has developed which provides for the development of the Inter-city sector only through technical innovation designed to produce high speed and high service quality. This seems to have arisen through an evolutionary process rather than as a consequence of any formal analysis of the whole of the passenger business, based on the theoretical framework described in chapter 2. This is not to say that the decisions are incorrect. Indeed it would be impossible to be dogmatic about the correctness of decisions. Decisions have always to be made without the advantage of hindsight and without perfect information. But the important thing to note is that decisions are more likely to be consistent one with another if they are examined within a framework that allows comparisons of alternative courses of action. In other words each decision can be viewed against others and evaluated on the basis of how they meet stated criteria for the present and for the future.

The main board and the boards of the individual businesses have not explicitly expressed their values and policies. Neither have the Department of Transport found it easy to be clear and definitive in this area. This was emphasised by the uncertainty in the 1976 Green Paper on Transport Policy,[4] which raised many questions in the values and policies area which have not been answered in the subsequent 1977 White Paper.[5] Confusion still exists, for example in such fundamental areas as quality and levels of service and acceptable levels of manpower productivity.

The situation is more serious on the question of objectives where the level of uncertainty is the cause of many problems. Objectives are set by government in one area only–the acceptable revenue account (profit-and-loss account) result. The *Transport Act 1962* specified that the board should have due regard to efficiency, economy and safety of operation. It also required a break-even situation on revenue account, taking one year with another.[6] This was varied by the *Transport Act 1968* to the extent that it permitted certain passenger grants to be taken into account in arriving at the revenue account balance as we saw in chapter 5. Again, it was required that the financial results should break even 'taking one year with another'.[7] This was varied by the *Railways Act 1974* which set up the P.S.O. grant procedure which again provided for the grant to be counted as a credit to the revenue account in arriving at the balance which should break even and added the requirement that the Railways passenger system should be run 'so as to provide a public service which is comparable generally with that provided by the Board at present'.[8] Thus, the essential ingredient of the 1962 Act remains intact–the break-even requirement, now after receipt of P.S.O., P.T.E. and Level Crossings grants. The non-passenger side of the Railways business and the non-railway businesses are required to break even without grants.

This stated objective has been incorporated into the corporate planning procedures but more as a constraint than as an objective. No major attempt in the six formal plans has been made to create formal objectives to achieve anything other than the break-even position. More generally, the plans prepared to date contain little regard to the development of rigorous objectives suitable for each business separately, or indeed, for parts of each business. Naturally, as a consequence of this there is little evidence of the 'goals' given in fig. 2.2. In the last year or so some consideration has been given to the creation of objectives for each of the railway passenger sectors (see discussion on White Paper 1977 in chapter 9) but to date such analyses have not been used in rail plans because they were not available. Indeed, they are not yet available and require detailed negotiation with government before they can be used in the later Rail Plans.

In these circumstances, one would expect the strategy area to be weak. This is not the case for some parts of the British Rail business and this is a credit to the British Rail planners. In the Railway business in particular, a great deal of effort has gone into developing a strategy for the Inter-city sector and, more recently, the freight business. The mechanism for this has been the commencement of sectoral strategic studies where each business is analysed into meaningful sectors for consideration of various alternatives designed to improve significantly the current situation, rather than meet a particular, discrete objective. However, in the non-railway businesses there has been little completed strategic activity of any note and their outline plans contain a sort of evolved strategy which is not particularly clearly defined.

The strategic studies procedure was extended in 1978 into Sealink U.K. Ltd, and it seems likely that all businesses will undertake such procedures within the next few years. During 1979 and continuing into 1980, however, the major strategic study is the Railway 'Passenger Strategic Study' which was commenced in 1978 and will deal with each of the passenger sectors both separately and collectively. A study of the parcels business commenced also in 1978. These require a deliberate effort to consider values, policies and objectives in conjunction with government, and it is clear that this degree of co-ordination is intended to exist. The White Paper 1977, which will be discussed in chapter 9, points to a government commitment to development of sectoral objectives, and this must improve the chances of success.

The British Railways Board decided in 1978 to place a great deal more emphasis on the continuation of the business and sector strategic studies. This decision resulted not just from the fact that the board felt that the effort already made had been worthwhile but because of dissatisfaction with the forecasts contained within the 1975, 1978 and 1979 Corporate Plans, particularly the Rail Plans. The board have described the 1978 and 1979 corporate/rail plans as corporate reviews rather than plans. This will remain the case until all the business and sector studies are completed.

In 1979 the board set up a new department to cater for this problem under the control of a director of strategic development (see fig. 4.3). In conjunction with the chief planning officer's department, they are charged with completing all the business and sector strategic studies, including a full review of electrification and the prospects for a Channel tunnel.

It may well be considered by some that it is regrettable that after nine years of corporate planning British Rail is not further ahead in strategic terms. We have some sympathy with that view but would mention that in such a difficult area and with problems of relating to government's changing requirements this is not too surprising.

The really strong and most sophisticated area in corporate planning is the production of the outline plans of the businesses; these represent the major part of the Corporate/Rail Plans effort. There is a great deal of interdepartmental co-operation in their production. They contain detailed analyses of an expected outcome in physical and financial terms, with an associated investment requirement. They are determined usually by using the modular forecasting approach discussed in chapter 3 starting with a marketing specification and ending with a financial evaluation. This procedure, because of its detailed analysis requirement, can take up to nine months to complete in the Railway business.

Until recently, the outline plans have been presented to the main board almost as final plans for approval, despite the lack of strategic refinement, on a sort of 'take it or leave it' basis. This has given the main board little time to produce any real effect except as part of the next annual planning cycle. This problem arose particularly in connection with the 1975 Corporate Plan, where its Rail Plan was evidently unacceptable in financial terms and did not become a formal document as a consequence. This was because the P.S.O. grant was seen to be rising too quickly and the freight/parcels loss declining too slowly.

The processes and actions suggested in chapter 2 to be important in the determination of action plans is largely missing in practice. Since 1970, there has been a tendency to move straight from 'outline plan' to first year budget without an action plan being prepared, the only exception being the use of a detailed investment programme. British Rail hopes soon to rectify this omission, but the advent of the P.S.O. cash limit has prompted the earlier preparation of a partial substitute system known as 'budget objectives' covering the expectation in year one of the plan. These have been determined at headquarters level and are intended to serve as early provisional budgets for one year and as a criterion for measuring the acceptability of the budgets completed about six months later. They are completely in line with the first year of the outline plan but cannot represent an adequate substitute for action plans.

The budgetary control procedures in British Rail are comprehensive and seem to fulfil the final stages of the corporate planning process as set out in chapter 2. However, monitoring is entirely against the budget only because there is no action plan to be monitored, except as we have noted in respect of investment which is monitored successfully.

In summary, it may be said that the practical response of British Rail to the general theory of corporate planning outlined in chapter 2 has been mixed. The major differences lie in the fields of values and policies which have not received much attention and of strategy where progress has been slow. Associated with these problems is the lack of attention–so far–to the development of internal objectives and goals both for British Rail as a whole and for each of its businesses. Also, the partial absence of action plans is a significant departure from the theory. On the credit side, however, we have observed the considerable effort in the development of strategy (although still far from fully developed), outline plans and the feedback and control exercised through the budgetary control system.

The question which must be asked is whether the theory outlined needs some modification or the implementation needs improvement. We consider that both considerations apply as we shall now explain.

British Rail, like other nationalised industries, is subject to considerable influence from the sponsoring government department and other government departments. This influence is embodied in statutes, rules and regulations, direct instructions, standards and monitoring arrangements. They create an atmosphere which severely restricts the board from feeling that it could develop values and policies as the corporate planning theory would suggest. This is taken further on the question of objectives where a minimum financial objective is laid down by statute and the level of the P.S.O. grant is prescribed by cash limit. This has led to the B.R.B. not determining its own objectives or any subdivision of them.

To some extent, the general theory outlined needs modifying. It is not appropriate to assume that the B.R.B. should assess its own values, policies and objectives, regarding those imposed from above as constraints. The influences are too far-reaching for that. Instead, it is suggested that these influences should be regarded more as minimum requirements and that the B.R.B. should make a conscious effort to extend them, particularly producing realistic and detailed objectives against which a strategy can be prepared. Naturally, these objectives would need to be agreed with the Department of Transport.

In doing this, it would seem sensible to adapt the theory further and confirm that each business has its own corporate plan. It is not really practical to prepare an overall strategy which might have the effect of improving one business at the expense of another. This is because of the unusual circumstances of British Rail, whereby each business has its own legal existence and its own set of government influences. Further, the B.R.B. is prevented from diversification to any significant degree and is faced with the task of developing each business separately without much competitive strategic interaction. This opinion was apparently held by Cooper Brothers in that their report regards each business plan as the main planning mechanism.

However, one of the main weaknesses in the strategy area, already mentioned, has been the lack of direct involvement of the main board with business plans being submitted to them on a 'take it or leave it basis'. It is considered essential that they be in a position to make a more positive contribution during the strategy stage, particularly if they adopt the suggested improvements in the objective stage. This requires rapid progress in the strategic studies activities and the agreement of strategy and its approximate assessed outcome well before the outline plans are prepared.

The procedures required for outline plans require little further comment but the determination of 'action plans' should be tackled urgently. The outline plans are not, and should not be required to be, a detailed programme of events. They are expected outcomes giving such information as resource expectations at each year end and during the specified period–say five years. In order that this outcome may be achieved, it is necessary to schedule all significant events and ensure that all parties at the appropriate levels are aware of what is required to be done. These are action plans. British Rail attend to this in the

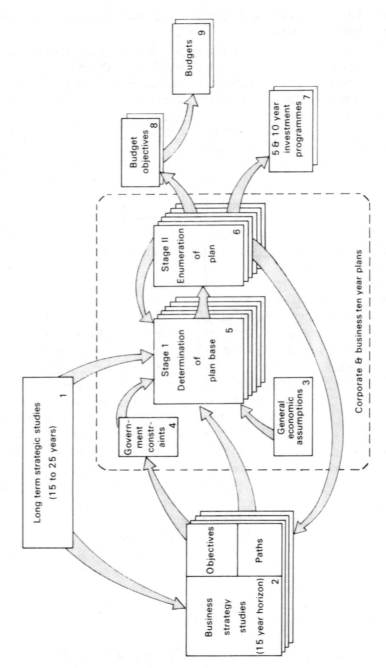

Fig. 6.2 The planning process–British Rail

investment field only but largely ignore the other significant features such as terminal closures, productivity schemes, train service alterations, etc. All of these are taken into account, implicitly, in the outline plans, but they are not converted into a detailed action plan. In this area it is considered that the theory outlined is sound but the practice is deficient.

The budget procedures are considered to be very sound and also the special 'budget objectives' arrangements, except that they should be tied in with action plans and not be loosely connected with the first year of the outline plan. However, it is considered that the feedback arrangements should be extended to monitor performance against all levels–particularly the outline plan and the action plan–and not merely against the one-year budget. This will enable corrective action to be taken at the appropriate level.

British Rail management has given consideration to the weaknesses in the procedures which they recognise as existing. To conclude this section we will outline their findings and comment as necessary. The proposals which have been developed during the last year or so represent the revision of the corporate planning procedures to create a system which is summarised in the B.R.B. model given in fig. 6.2.

The essential new ingredient of this procedure is the recognition of the need for greater involvement of the main board in the development of strategy. It is considered that this can best be achieved by adopting a 'two-stage' approach within the annual planning cycle with forecasts being prepared at each stage. Stage I has been identified as the 'determination of plan base' which relates to the development of sub-strategic options with an outline evaluation. This assumes that the major elements of the strategy will have been settled at the 'business and sector strategy studies' stage and already agreed at Board and Department of Transport level. Stage II is the 'enumeration of plan' which is the final 'outline plan' which follows main board and business board discussion on the Stage I information. This arrangement, which was applied to the 1979 Rail Plan, deals adequately with the criticism made earlier concerning main board involvement. Also, as mentioned earlier, the strategy studies concept is considered to be an excellent idea in that it enables significant changes of direction to be properly considered. However, it is not clear why this should be followed by objectives, and it would appear from this evidence that British Rail is not wholly ready to grasp the nettle in the values, policies and objectives areas. The implication of the White Paper 1977 in this direction will be considered in chapter 9 where it will be seen that objectives at least may soon be tackled further.

The weaknesses discussed in connection with 'action plans' are not solved within the model of the proposed revised procedures, which ratify existing processes. However, it is understood that British Rail management has had second thoughts in this area and further improvements are being developed.

All in all, although progress is slow, it is encouraging to note that British Rail are actively engaged in correcting theoretical deficiencies. There can be little doubt that they will remain in the forefront of developments in corporate planning within the public sector. In the long run this must be good for the industry and the taxpayer who foots all residual bills. However, readers may wish to judge this from a consideration of the strategic and tactical issues rather than the comparison of theoretical concepts and applied procedures. This will be covered in chapter 9, where a number of topical issues will be considered within a corporate/financial planning context.

Before moving on to consider financial planning practice in the light of the theory expounded in chapter 3 and the corporate planning practice already discussed, let us have a brief look at the use made of computer 'corporate models' thus completing the comparison with chapter 2. British Rail are quite advanced in this area, having established a simple computer model in 1973 and now being in the process of preparing a comprehensive computer model. Both models are designed to deal with the production of the 'outline plans' for the Railways business and for testing sub-strategic options.

The smaller model is known as P.L.A.T.O. Its function is to manipulate the financial and physical data input from the Rail Plan by the application of variations in selected key variables. It is designed to answer relatively minor 'what if' questions and will not deal with major variations or variations with known complex consequential effects.

The bigger model will take a further year or so to design and implement. Its function is to deal with the whole of the present manual process—the documentation for which has been reviewed to facilitate the process—by computerising all of the procedures. This is likely to be achieved using a computer time-sharing agency with a computer terminal already installed in B.R. headquarters. The benefits of the proposed system will be enormous and relate to the reduction in time spent on producing the outline plan and the ability to process many complex variations to the data, i.e. options for consideration. To ensure that the functional arrangements presently existing are not lost, arrangements are being made to ensure that the functional planners use the model for their part of the process, thus maintaining the modular approach.

6.2 Financial planning practice in British Rail

To examine financial planning practice in British Rail following a section of corporate planning practice in British Rail could be extremely repetitious. This is not merely because financial planning is a vital part of corporate planning but because, in respect of British Rail, it is the entire area of practice. As we suggested in chapter 3, within most organisations the determination of financial objectives and a strategy for their achievement is of paramount importance within the corporate plan. However, one would expect that if full corporate planning exists, this would manifest itself in the existence of non-financial objectives and a strategy covering their achievement. These non-financial objectives would be in such areas as market share, market location, product service, quality and range and personnel improvements (e.g. pay, conditions, local employment situation, etc.). Naturally, these objectives and related strategies must be compatible.

Within British Rail, the limited targets which exist in these areas are not formal objectives in themselves, but evidence of physical results which must be achieved if the limited financial objectives are to be met. We have seen that there are weaknesses in the area of financial objectives also, but at least they form the reason, other than that corporate planning is fashionable, why the corporate planning procedures exist at all. Thus, we are bound to observe that within the theories outlined in chapters 2 and 3, the corporate planning within British Rail is entirely financial planning. This is not too surprising given the nature and dimension of British Rail's financial circumstances. Every organisation starting out on the corporate planning road has to tackle its main problems first and not try to be too sophisticated from the start. Furthermore, in most organisations, financial plans in one shape or form have existed for many years, and it is understandable that they should form a major structural input into any subsequent corporate planning routine.

Thus, the detail of the corporate planning practice given in the previous section is also a summary of the financial planning practice. There is quite a lot more to add but the comments that follow apply more to some of the detail of the procedures than to the structural relationships with the model in fig. 2.2.

6.2.1 Forecasting

We mentioned in the forecasting section of chapter 3 that forecasting is linked not only to the financial aspects of the model in fig. 2.2 but also to the non-financial aspects. Indeed, forecasting is critical to the whole process. At the outline plan stage of the model, British Rail follows the process given in fig. 3.1. The financial evaluation involves integrating the forecasts of the modules taken sequentially. Looking at the Railways business as an example, the marketing specification is built up using the forecast plan assumptions mentioned in the previous section and market research information obtained by a thorough survey of prospects, obtained at headquarters, regional and divisional levels. This provides the background information required for the production specification, which is determined by extrapolating base year production data (i.e. resources and train/traction miles) on the basis of these assumptions. This extrapolation also takes into account changes in production requirements consequent upon many other issues including predicted variations in the nature and age of the resources (investment and scrapping), productivity, staff conditions of service and reorganisation proposals.

Both the marketing and production specifications determine the content of the investment specification and a measure of negotiation takes place to agree a reasonable split between the three Railway businesses. This negotiation does not follow the strict theoretical principle of proceeding with projects producing the best net present values because of the need to replace old assets and the social needs implicit in the P.S.O. arrangements, but is more of a subjective assessment. There has been relatively little disagreement within the Railway business because the freight and parcels businesses make relatively modest demands on the capital investment portion of the cash ceiling and the passenger business takes the balance.

The revenue investment proposals of the civil engineer and the signal and telecommunications engineer together and the business requirements for capital investment involve much more difficult negotiation. This is generally settled by debate at the rail planning group and subsidiary meetings where a 'share some of the misery' solution is established. The main criteria in this case, however, are the essential nature of large parts of the revenue investment, i.e. track and signalling renewal. The production of the investment specification usually results in some recycling of both the marketing and production specifications which would have been regarded as temporary until that stage.

The manpower specification is prepared from the resource data contained within the production specifications with the addition of administrative requirements outlined by all departments. This requirement is then converted into an 'anticipated actual' by recognition of the existing and predicted labour market situation. This part of the process is presently not very sophisticated and could rightly be described as a 'broad brush' approach. However, British Rail hope to improve this by disaggregating the forecasts to geographical areas and producing labour market comparisons on these smaller figures. This will facilitate a more detailed supply and demand analysis leading to improved recruitment and training programmes.

The financial evaluation of these specifications is the final stage in the round of main work in connection with the 'outline plan'. The evaluation uses information obtained from each of the other stages to provide information for the extrapolation of costs and receipts. The receipts come straight from marketing specification. The forecast costs are calculated in considerable detail by the nature of the expenditure. These are forecast for the business as a whole and for the sectors and sub-sectors beneath. In order that this may be done, it is necessary for the other specifications to contain information in that degree of detail. The manpower information is used initially on a requirement basis and some regard is then paid to the 'estimated actuals'. This adjustment relates only to the assessment of the number of staff predicted not to be required beyond the level that would be catered for by natural wastage. This part of the financial evaluation is known as the 'disengagement costs'. No attempt is presently made to deal with the more general differences between the manpower 'requirement' and 'anticipated actual', since it is argued that the cost projections vary roughly in line with the requirements. However, this assertion is also being studied in more detail in an attempt to improve future procedures.

The output of the financial evaluation is geared to the need for a profit-and-loss account for each business and 'contribution' (i.e.

receipts minus direct expenses only) for each sector and sub-sector. Tables and appendices are produced for inclusion in the Rail Plan document and supported by physical data forecasts obtained from the other specifications. These all give credibility and understanding to the financial forecasts. Generally speaking the Rail Plans (and those of the other businesses) cover the current 'base' year, each of the following five years and a snapshot view of the tenth year.

Most of the financial forecasts are prepared in 'constant' prices, relating to the average price level of the base year, as seen in the budget for that year. In addition the summary forecasts are also converted to future prices by the use of predicted inflation indices derived from a retail prices index forecast. However, bearing in mind the difficulty of interpreting figures in future prices, the accent is on the constant price forecasts. These constant price forecasts are made more difficult to assess than one might imagine by the fact that predicted receipts and costs will not vary in line merely with predicted inflation and volume changes. To overcome this, the financial evaluation procedures acknowledge that there will be a level of real price increases or decreases and real staff costs escalation. No account is presently taken of real non-staff cost increases although recent evidence suggests that this should be done. Further, the most recent evaluations, which recognise some strategic changes, base year changes and assumption changes, recognise that to arrive at true constant pricing, costs which cannot rise with inflation must be discounted to provide accurate forecasts. This applies to parts of the depreciation and interest calculations, where a complex evaluation model has been devised to produce the forecasts.

The bulk of this financial evaluation takes place at headquarters level for each business. The Railway regions and divisions and the equivalent structures in the other businesses are not closely involved in the process. Communication of the contents of the outline plans has also been severely restricted for reasons of commercial secrecy and industrial relations sensitivity. Coupled with the absence of an action plan, this places the lower management levels in a largely uninformed situation. It might be argued, therefore, that this discourages middle management in that they are unable to see the entire logic of any situation. Thus, while the lower management levels are intimately involved in the budgeting process they may feel that they are not encouraged to think wider or longer term than the immediate future. British Rail is aware of this potential danger and hopes to overcome some of these fears, in connection with future plans, although no arrangements have yet been made.

Forecasting also features largely in the strategy stage of the process. Although there seems to be a lack of a clear set of objectives, British Rail planners have produced an outline scenario of the economic and transport environment up to the year 2000, known as the 'Long Term Strategic Study'. This has not yet enabled them to produce an overall strategy to change or get the best out of that scenario, but it is a step in the right direction. The forecasting procedures used are qualititative in nature. The strategic study is regarded as a prime input to the more detailed sectoral strategic evaluations.

We saw in the corporate planning section of this chapter that the main work to date in this area has covered the development of a strategy for the Inter-city sector of the passenger business, a strategy for the freight business and the commencement of a sectoral strategic study for the rest of passenger business sectors. The forecasting procedures used in this process are almost identical with the description of the outline plan procedures just described. This seems quite sensible, given that the overall scenario is achieved by a more 'naive' type of forecasting.

As was true for the outline plan forecasting process, the first forecasting stage, prior to the preparation of the marketing specification, is the determination of planning assumptions. These apply equally to the strategic studies and basically cover economic growth, inflation, real wage escalation and investment ceilings. However, for British Rail there is also a vital unwritten assumption which has a significant effect on current planning forecasts. This is the assumption that there will be no compulsory redundancy. The disengagements costs forecasts, mentioned earlier, allow for this assumption where the need arises. This means that the accent is on natural wastage and voluntary redundancy. This assumption is born of many difficult reorganisation and manpower reduction consultation problems over the years and the attitudes struck by the railway unions. We will discuss this issue further in chapter 9.

6.2.2 Budgeting and budgetary control

The application of budgeting and budgetary control within British Rail is very much in line with the theoretical explanation given in chapter 3. The only major difference relates to the stated absence of an 'action plan', apart from the investment programme. It has already been noted that this is a significant omission. Without action plans there cannot be full co-ordination of the budget with the outline plan because the outline plan would not contain sufficient detailed information to allow this to happen. Instead, it would contain anticipated annual and year-end forecasts assuming groups of events which would need to be programmed in much greater detail.

We mentioned earlier that British Rail management have only recently recognised the existence of this problem and chose to regard the forecast result of the first year of each outline plan as a criterion for measuring the efficiency of the budget for that year. To overcome the problem of changing price levels and to ensure that the figures are up to date in other respects also, they produce a new version of that first year of the plan, described as the 'budget objectives'. Until 1979 they related to the Railway business but have now been extended to cover the other businesses, pending longer term development of action plans. These budget objectives are themselves prepared in broad terms. The detailed actions are only recorded in the budget itself, which is built up from ground level. They are prepared at headquarters level with no lower level involvement on the costs side but with some up-to-date market research information on the receipts side. The purpose of the budget objectives which were introduced in 1976 was not to overcome the absence of an action plan. That problem has only recently been recognised. Instead, they are required to give advance warning of cash limit problems and to give Railway region general managers a clear idea of the net results that are expected of them. To achieve this, the figures are disaggregated over regions using outline plans data which are often insufficient for that purpose. This results in a measure of broad allocation, particularly in the area of staff costs and manpower numbers.

The arrangement does seem to work for the purpose for which it was designed. It may be inadequate in full financial planning context, but it represents a very clear downwards communication of part of the outline plan and an equally positive response. However, the Railway regions regard it more as an arbitrary target setting exercise than a partial communication of the Rail Plan.

The budgeting and budgetary control procedures use cost, receipt and profit centres. Again, using the Railways business as an example, receipts and cost centre structures are extensively used. A pyramid situation exists at the four management levels identifying responsibility for both receipts and costs. Each receipt and cost centre is of a single function, thus permitting the aggregation of receipt by business, and costs by spending department (see structure in fig. 4.3) within headquarters, regional and divisional levels. Thus, the 'functional' officers at each level are fully involved in the budgeting process as well as the chief executive (railways), regional general managers and divisional managers.

The method of recording receipts is known as the receipts classi-fication. This divides passenger receipts over such headings as full fares, reduced fares and seasons, freight receipts over commodities (e.g. iron and steel, earths and stones) and parcels receipts also over commodities (e.g. newspapers, general parcels and mail order con-tracts). The method of recording costs is by the usual types of expend-iture (known as 'source' accounting within B.R.) meaning such items as wages, salaries, national insurance, electricity and hired cartage.

All of this is fairly usual and straightforward; the complexities arise when this information is converted into profit centres, sectors and sub-sectors, which we can now proceed to describe under the same heading as used in chapter 3–Aspects of costing.

6.2.3 Aspects of costing

This section will describe British Rail's position on costing procedures and the monitoring of costs and revenues through profit centres. One of the major problems in any railway organisation is that of dis-tinguishing between the costs of one part of the business and another. This problem is recognised as one of internal parts of the business having 'joint costs' as a result of sharing facilities such as track. British Rail has established an extensive profit centre system within the business sector system of the Railways business, already outlined. The structure of the business/sector/profit centre system, for the Railway business, is given in table 6.1. It illustrates that British Rail has found it necessary to create sub-sectors, within the sectors men-tioned so far, to provide information for major groups of passenger services on the passenger side and commodities on the freight side.

At first sight the planning information structures in table 6.1 may look too detailed for efficient financial planning, when run in parallel with a budgetary control system. However, this is not the case because the Railways business is a large complex concern which needs to be broken down into meaningful parts when preparing and monitoring

Table 6.1   **British Rail–railways business sector and profit centre structure**

Total		Railway total	
Businesses	Passenger	Freight	Parcels
Sectors	Inter-city L. & S.E. P.T.E. Other Provincial	Train load Less than train load	—

Sub-sectors	Passenger service groups
	  Inter-city 13
	  L. & S.E. 13
	  P.T.E. 2
	  Other Provincial 4
	                      ――
	                      32
		Freight commodities
		  T.L. 12
		  L.T.T.L. 2
		             ――
		             14
			—

Profit centres*	Passenger services
	  Inter-city 97
	  L. & S.E. 63
	  P.T.E. 75
	  Other Provincial 86
	                     ―――
	                     321
		Freight services
		  Selected train load
		    only 295
			—

* Budget analysis only.

outline plans and perhaps action plans, eventually. Each part of the business has its own characteristics which require separate examination. However they are not free-standing, and there are strong interrelationships within and between some of the Railways businesses.

Let us look at table 6.1 further and discuss the extent of the financial planning process which applies to each section. A primary observation to make is that the Rail Plan production procedure (which we have described as being basically the 'outline plan' stage of the model in fig. 2.2) covers all of the sections apart from the profit centres. The profit centres represent a redistribution of the budgeted costs and receipts over the services. The budgets are prepared for one year only and not for the remaining years of the 'outline plan'. The passenger profit centres cover the whole of the passenger business. This is not the case for the freight business because the number of services is so large that it is necessary to select the most important and allow the balance of receipts and costs to be recorded in a residual profit centre known as 'system freight'. This residue includes the whole of the 'Less than Train Load' sector. All of the other sections relate to the 'rail plan' processes and forecasts are prepared for the whole of the plan period, i.e. the base year (budget), each of the following five years and the tenth year.

Table 6.1 shows that there is no analysis of the forecasts of the parcels business. This is because it has been established that it is extremely difficult to divide the costs of that business over sectors, commodities or services. However, the parcels sectoral strategic study will make inroads in this area. Most of the parcels traffic is carried on passenger trains and a great deal of the rest is carried in composite trains thus creating a very high degree of joint costs. There is a possibilty that part of the newspapers traffic could be made into a number of profit centres because separate trains are provided for part of the traffic. However, no arrangements have been made to do this and all of the 'outline plans' to date treat the parcels business as an entity which cannot be subdivided at the profit contribution level. The receipts are, however, subdivided over the commodities.

Table 6.2

	Passenger	*Freight*	*Parcels*
Receipts			
Deduct Direct costs			
Movements			
Terminals			
Contribution			
Deduct Indirect costs			
Track and signalling			
Administration			
Operating profit			
Add Ancillary income			
Deduct Interest			
Grant (P.S.O.)			
Profit/Loss			

Only at the business level are total costs compared with total receipts to produce a profit situation. The summary layout of the profit-and-loss account is shown in table 6.2. It will be noticed that the distribution between so called direct (those which can be directly related to and which vary with output) and indirect (those which cannot be directly related to or vary in relation with output) costs is fairly similar to the specific and joint costs given in chapter 3. The two are not the same, however, because there are elements of the indirect costs which are specific to the three businesses and, to a lesser extent, to the sectors, sub-sectors and profit centres beneath. An example of this would be the maintenance of a stretch of track which is only used for the freight business. Conversely, there are elements of the direct costs that are joint.

The profit centre, sub-sector and sector forecasts are presently made on the basis of a 'contribution' level only, recognising that the indirect costs are mostly joint and are, therefore, incapable of being spread other than through the use of meaningless allocation techniques such as those discussed in chapter 3. This has produced an interesting dilemma. During 1975 and much of 1976 the Department of Transport were constantly pressing British Rail to allocate the passenger indirect costs to establish the sector spread of P.S.O. grant. Indeed, British Rail reluctantly did so, producing figures which the government used in the 1976 Green Paper (see chapter 9). However, the B.R.B. were able later to convince them of the uselessness of such information and such allocations are not now made. This is contrary to general practice within most other European railways where the neat and tidy full allocation process is taken to extremes, often down to services. B.R.B. officers have been trying to change this to prevent such procedures featuring in standard accounting practices which are being established by the U.I.C., as discussed further in chapter 7. This is now meeting with some success in theoretical agreement but with little practical effect to date.

The distribution of joint costs among the three businesses in total has not required a resort to arbitrary allocations because of the effect of the *Railways Act 1974*. This created arrangements whereby the freight and parcels businesses taken together (under the title of the non-passenger business) would be charged only with their avoidable costs. This has been interpreted as the whole of their direct costs plus an avoidable share of their indirect costs. Thus the passenger business, and therefore the P.S.O. grant, has become the residual legatee of the remaining indirect costs. The splitting of the avoidable indirect costs between freight and parcels has been reasonably achieved because although the sum of their individual avoidable costs does not equal the whole, which has to be determined under the Act, the difference is negligible and has been spread on a 'fair share' basis.

The B.R.B. is fully aware of the fact that their direct costs and indirect costs differ from specific costs and joint costs, respectively, and are taking action to move over to the specific/common/joint basis, which they have used since 1970 in minor costing exercises. This will enable them to establish sector and profit centre contributions which are theoretically more correct. However, they may try to keep the direct/indirect split as well, although this would seem to be superfluous. They recognise that what is specific at one level may not be so at a lower level and will be setting out their documentation accordingly. In making these arrangements they have identified a significant level of common costs which vary with output and can be associated with sectors, sub-sectors and profit centres by work measurement. Train crew costs are a prime example because flexibility of operation can mean that a train crew can be engaged in work associated with more than one sector, sub-sector or business during a working day. At the end they are treated as specific costs by work measurement.

It is intended that the change of procedure will be introduced in 1980 and will represent a considerable step forward in the accurate measurement of profit contributions. This will not only facilitate the financial planning process in its forecasting stages but also in the feedback. At the moment, the entire financial feedback is through the responsibility budgeting system. From 1980 it is proposed to produce 'actual' profit centre results to compare with the profit centre budgets. Whilst it has not yet been considered, this will undoubtedly lead to the longer-term production of sector and sub-sector results. The feedback system will then be much more complete than the current situation, whereby the profit and profit contribution results are reported at the business level only.

The longer-term aim of the B.R.B. is to move to an avoidable costs/receipts approach at the business and sector level (not at the profit centre level) to get over the problem of having such a large level of costs (joint costs) being treated as not capable of being associated with these levels. Also, it will identify an element of joint costs (which may be large) that represents that portion which is not avoidable in the absence of each sector individually, which has been described as the 'basic facility cost'.[9] This system, which is discussed further in chapter 9, would produce figures according to the layout in table 6.3.

Table 6.3

	Passenger				Freight	Parcels	Total
	Inter-city	*L. & S.E.*	*P.T.E.*	*Other*			
Avoidable receipts							
Deduct Avoidable costs							
Specific/Common							
Joint							
Total							
Sector profit contribution							
Basic facility cost							—
Loss before P.S.O.							
Grant–P.S.O.							—
Profit after P.S.O.							—

There can be little doubt that this procedure represents a considerable step forward in the proper measurement of sector profit contributions which will considerably help the planning procedures.

　　The B.R.B. are very much at the forefront of developments in this area and are keen to make their costing procedures as useful and efficient as possible. Naturally they are conscious of the need to provide public information as well as that required for internal decision-making. Concern in this area has led them to produce and publish an excellent booklet entitled *Measuring Cost and Profitability in British Rail,* which deals with the issues used in this section in some detail and with useful diagrams.[10] It covers the problems of assessing second order avoidability and dual avoidability, discussed in chapter 3, suggesting that British Rail are taking this issue very seriously and will produce results of high technical quality.

6.2.4 Investment appraisal

The application of investment appraisal in British Rail is not fully in line with the theory outlined in chapter 3. We have seen how investment is limited to 'ceiling' figures laid down by government. Ideally, this would mean that British Rail should select the best projects within those limits using the D.C.F. approach. Unfortunately, however, more than half of the investment is classified as revenue and even more of that classified as capital is of an essential replacement nature and is not measured in terms of net present value. The D.C.F. approach is only used fully for projects of a development nature, e.g. the high-speed train where it is necessary to rank various options. In such projects, the motivation is not merely to replace worn out assets but to introduce far superior assets designed to produce improved cash flows. In such circumstances a test discount rate of 10% has applied to constant price cash flows, in accordance with the requirements of Cmnd 3437. Changes have been made recently, however, to allow for a government 'required rate of return' and this is discussed in chapter 9.

To overcome this problem, British Rail place great reliance on their business plans as being the overall means of justifying the investment programme. The overriding principle is to satisfy the Department of Transport and B.R.B. management about the forecast plan results and the investment programme as part of the plan. No attempt is made to use the D.C.F. procedures by forecasting the cash flows after investment in comparison with the adverse change in cash flow which will result from non-investment in those assets requiring essential replacement. All schemes with an outlay of £2 m or over are subject to approval by the Department of Transport officials. All such schemes are submitted for approval, but a detailed investigation usually takes place only in the case of larger proposals (usually over £10 m) or those selected as being of special interest.

6.2.5 Pricing

The attitude towards pricing within British Rail is very clear-cut. The object of the exercise is to charge prices as close to the market price as can be reasonably indentified and obtained. This approach used to be applied in the form of across-the-board increases for much of each business up to 1967. However, since then, largely under the influence of the prices and incomes report on passenger fares,[11] the individual traffic flows and contracts have been separately examined to apply the market pricing on as selective a basis as thought feasible.

Little attempt is made to assess short-run or long-run marginal costs to determine price levels. Indeed, costs seldom enter into the equation at all. The prime concern is maximisation of revenue by applying selective price increases a little short of the level where resistance would escalate to a level which produced a negligible return. However, on the freight side, particularly, costing exercises are sometimes undertaken to identify the specific and common costs of specific flows to facilitate the price making process. In such cases costs are used to determine minimum acceptable prices for traffic subject to individual contract.

This sounds a little harsh, but it is a direct result of having financial obligations which are difficult to attain. We will discuss this problem further in chapter 9.

SEVEN

B.R. Relationships with Government and Their Effect on Corporate/Financial Planning

The purpose of this chapter is to consider British Rail's relationships with the government in this country and the possible effect of European legislation on the transport scene. We will outline the various statutory frameworks that have influenced the parameters of many of the British Rail corporate plans. We also discuss other less tangible issues which provide some additional complexities in corporate and financial planning in British Rail.

It should be noted that although much of the historical information given in the first part of this chapter tends to be critical of the relationship between British Rail and government, there are very good reasons for our stating that we consider that the situation has improved in the last two or three years. In particular, the development of business and sector strategic studies with the growing involvement of civil servants from the Department of Transport must augur well for future relationships. Also, the development of sector targets, which will be dealt with in chapter 9, may prove most rewarding for both parties. Above all, however, it should be noted that the spirit of co-operation now existing is considered to be much higher than at any time described in this chapter.

This does not mean that the 1979 Corporate/Rail Plan can be regarded as a joint proposal. As mentioned in chapter 6, the board is not sufficiently convinced about its strategic content for that situation to arise and have retitled it the 1979 Corporate Review. However, as long as the Department of Transport is willing and able to participate in the development of strategy, the chances of creating an approved Corporate/Rail Plan must be high.

Most of the influences have come from government within the

United Kingdom. The first part of this chapter will consider these in some detail and will attempt to distinguish between the formal and informal relationships which exist and comment on their effectiveness as seen from within British Rail.

Another set of influences from government come from Europe. Clearly, with Britain becoming a full member of the E.E.C. these have increased. Section 2 of this chapter will examine some of the most important pieces of European legislation which relate to financial planning. Even before this, however, British Rail was closely involved with other railway systems in Europe. It seems reasonably obvious that this was a natural development of rail traffic travelling through a number of countries and thus agreements had to be reached about allocation of costs and revenues among the various railway companies. The body that integrated the discussions with respect to such issues was the Union Internationale Chemin-de-fer (U.I.C.).

7.1 U.K. government

In theory a nationalised industry's relationship with a government department should be related to direction and discussion of long-term objectives, according to national policies. In addition there should be some form of monitoring related to the demands which that particular nationalised industry makes upon the nation's purse.

Railways form part of the larger transport scene in the United Kingdom. From the early days of nationalisation much emphasis has been placed on the need for some measure of co-ordination of transport resources and the idea that the long-term objectives for a nationalised railway system should be part of a co-ordinated transport plan. One of the unfortunate features of the transport scene has been the lack of agreement on a national transport plan, specifically whether there should be free competition among all modes of transport or whether road and rail should be seen as complementary, with some central direction of traffics in the best interests of the economic use of the national resources. Whatever the reasons, political, idealistic, theoretical or practical, no consensus has been reached on such a plan and it is not surprising, therefore, that no long-term objectives have been derived by government for the nation's railway system.

Various attempts have been made; the 1967 Joint Steering Group, set up by Barbara Castle, was one. It ultimately led to Cmnd 3439 *Railway Policy*[1] and hence the *1968 Transport Act*.[2] There was also the Railway Policy Review, initiated by the railways themselves in 1973. All of these have been honest attempts to set or, in the latter case, encourage *inter alia* the setting of positive objectives for British Rail, which have unfortunately come to nought.

In chapter 4, some indication is given in fig. 4.2 of the main relationships with government. There are direct influences that emanate from the sponsoring Secretary of State and his department. There are less direct links with other Ministries and the Treasury. Finally, there are the links with Parliament through committees such as the Select Committee for Nationalised Industries, the Public Accounts Committee and, ultimately, the Cabinet itself. Obviously, these relationships vary in intensity and in the amount of influence that they can and do bring to bear on the objectives of British Railways.

The influence that the Cabinet is able to bring to bear is, of course, paramount whether it be as a decision relating to a particular national-ised industry or a general pronouncement relating to the public sector. The influence of the various reports of the Select Committee on Nationalised Industries is perhaps less easy to determine. Cer-tainly, the First Report from the Select Committee on Nationalised Industries, Session 1967–68, on Ministerial Control of the National-ised Industries,[3] in three massive volumes, is a fruitful source for the student on how influence and control was seen to be exerted in theory and practice. It is interesting to note that the Select Committee in its report chapter XVIII 'What Has Gone Wrong' chose to quote, with evident belief, the then Railway Board Chairman, Sir Stanley Raymond, who said '. . . we have not got yet the proper relationship between the nationalised industries, their sponsoring departments and the government'.[4] Perhaps the only comment that is necessary is to refer the reader to the N.E.D.O. report which was able to comment eight years later that '. . . the functions of the Department of the Environment in relation to the Board are overlapping and confused. What each expects of the other is ambiguous or unrealistic'[5]–*plus ça change*. It is certainly difficult for people in the nationalised industries to perceive the direct influence of the select committees although it is possible that the 1977 Select Committee on British Rail[6] may eventu-ally have some effect on the legislation which follows the 1977 White Paper.[7]

Since nationalisation, British Rail has been heavily influenced by a series of Acts which have played a great part in defining the statutory framework of its existence and its relationship with government and the Civil Service. It is considered useful to make passing mention of the more important parts of the various Acts which are, briefly, as follows.

The 1947 Act,[8] as might be expected, had as its main theme the integration of all transport activities on a national basis. However, it did not take long for the practical difficulties of such a task to make themselves manifest. The 1953 Act[9] deleted the principle of integration from the statutory duties of the then Transport Commission; in fact it removed the Commission's powers and obligations in relation to area passenger schemes and required it to dispose of its road haulage businesses so painfully integrated in the previous six years. Instead, integration was replaced with competition, with some element of co-ordination in respect of the activities of London passenger transport. Three years later, the 1956 Act[10] allowed the Commission to retain part of the road haulage business as it was felt, at that time, that to remove the final stage of a journey by rail, i.e. the delivery side, was inconsistent.

After a further six years had elapsed, the *1962 Transport Act*[11] required the Commission to transfer to the Transport Holding Company the whole of the road haulage and road passenger business. As regards subsequent formulation of financial objectives, the requirement in the 1962 Act for the Board to break even on revenue account 'taking one year with another'[12] was to be a significant yardstick for the next decade and that was only modified in the 1968 Act to the extent that grant payments under sections 39, 40 and 56 were concerned.[13]

An interesting milestone was Cmnd 3437,[14] which was an attempt to set, amongst other things, criteria for investment in relation to all nationalised industries. But as the 1977 N.E.D.O. Report says,

'Only a limited proportion of investment in nationalised industries is subject to full investment appraisal using the test discount rate (T.D.R.) procedure of the 1967 White Paper. . . . In contrast with most other sponsor departments the Department of the Environment devotes comparatively large resources to appraisal of British Rail investment plans. This must to some extent require the greater dependence of British Rail on government financial support. However, detailed departmental scrutiny of individual projects by the Department's economist has probably been disproportionate in view of the unresolved differences in viewpoint between the department and corporation on the size of the rail network and related services required in the future. *In the absence of an agreed strategy related investment policy, the use of the T.D.R. and detailed economic appraisal of individual investment projects become relatively minor issues.'* (Author's emphasis).[15]

This is indeed a fair reflection of the actual position in British Rail where the additional complication arises that the bulk of investment requirements, more than 80% in the case of Railways, is occasioned by the need to replace existing assets. It will be obvious that without a strategy for expansion or reduction this must be so; although there arises the question of betterment, i.e. the improvements that arise from the replacement of life expired assets in more modern form, which is relevant in considering the financial criteria adopted for evaluation of corporate plans.

The *1968 Transport Act* stripped the last of the road vehicle fleets remaining with the Railways and transferred the sundries division and the newly developed freightliner business to the successor to the Transport Holding Company, the National Freight Corporation. Also embodied in the 1968 Act, in sections 10–20, were the seeds for the eventual disruption of the national railway system, if carried through to their logical conclusion. The creation of Passenger Transport Authorities with their executive arms the Passenger Transport Executives, in the main urban areas outside London, can be seen as either an enlightened attempt to give the people who pay a chance to express their views or an attack on a national system resulting in an uneasy agreement between the British Railways Board and the local politically appointed representatives, with sometimes dissimilar transport objectives.

The *Railways Act 1974*[16] endeavoured in the sections dealing with the public service obligation to respond to the parallel E.E.C. legislation[17] which had made mandatory support to passenger transport systems. However, one should note the general terms in which this was expressed in the Secretary of State's direction to the board:

'the British Railways Board shall, from 1 January 1975, operate their railway passenger system so as to provide a public service which is comparable generally with that provided by the Board at present'.[18]

Even to the casual reader it will be obvious that the successive pieces of legislation briefly mentioned above were hardly conducive to continuity of purpose in the minds of politicians or civil servants and, in fact, this ever changing legislative pattern serves as a pointer to the difficulty of the Transport Commission and later the Railways Board in its relationships with government. If one sets alongside this the varying cycle of national economic events and adds to it the apparently worsening financial results successively thrown up by British Rail, one can see that in the eyes of ministers and civil servants alike the Railways came to be regarded as one of the more awkward problem children.

This has been reflected in the statutory financial requirements and the non-statutory monitoring requirements imposed upon the Board throughout those years. In 1947, one of the most important of the specific ministerial powers was that:

'In framing programmes of reorganisation or development involving a substantial outlay on capital account, the Commission shall act on lines settled from time to time with the approval of the Minister.'[19]

This fairly general power was something which the Transport Commission shared with most of the other nationalised industries. However, the need for the permanent secretary to justify expenditure to the Public Accounts Committee, in his role as accounting officer, has meant that the Railways Board with its succession of deficit payments, subsidies, grant payments under the 1968 Act and, at present, the payments under the public service obligation and the recent freight support, has become increasingly enmeshed in the civil service toils. It has been placed in a very weak position to resist interference on the part of both politicians and civil servants, so much so that it led the N.E.D.O. report to say in its comments on accountability:

'In the case of British Railways the position is further complicated because of the wider statutory powers given to the Minister in the *1974 Railways Act* and the continuing subsidy situation which gives added emphasis to the permanent secretary's "accounting officer" role. The result is that the Department of Environment and British Railways are not in agreement about where the dividing line lies between each other's responsibilities.'[20]

How has this affected corporate and financial planning? We have seen in chapter 6 that corporate planning in a formal sense only emerged in the early 1970s in British Railways. Nonetheless government and civil service attitudes to the emergence of plans must surely have inevitably been conditioned by the long and arduous struggles which had already taken place over the 'Modernisation', 'Beeching' and other plans in the previous decades. With this in mind it is perhaps interesting to note the reception accorded to the various corporate plans that the Railways have prepared since the formation of a corporate planning department.

The First Corporate Plan, covering the five-year period 1971–5, was submitted to the Minister for Transport Industries on 30 December 1970. Whilst stressing the complexity of the task in preparing the plan the then Chairman, Sir Henry Johnson, was careful to point out that many problems defined in the process required further study. It was the hope of the board that, with this as a base document for discussion with the government and civil servants, many of these problems could be jointly tackled. Several months of intensive joint discussion, criticism and explanation were to follow, and in May 1971 the board were anticipating that this joint appraisal process would facilitate development of future plans. With the expressed intention of involving the Department from an early stage of their preparation, particularly on matters for which responsibility for long-term guidance could be regarded as the Department's responsibility, the possibility of improving future corporate plans seemed assured.

One very concrete result of the appraisal conducted on the First Corporate Plan was that whilst it showed evidence of considerable financial achievement with considerable potential for improvement, there was absolutely no assurance that the existing rail system could be made viable within the statutory framework of the *1968 Transport Act*. This was probably a 'watershed' in the Railway Board thinking about the financial viability of the organisation. It could also be said to be the beginning of a rift between the Railways Board and the civil servants. The latter still held the opinion that somewhere, almost like a needle in a haystack, was a viable railway and indeed in the months following May 1971 a considerable amount of effort went into financial evaluations of six different network sizes–in an attempt to find the 'needle'.

These studies were undertaken by a small team of Railways finance and planning officers. Not surprisingly, when they were considered in October of that year no viable railway had been discovered. Indeed the indications were that the transitional cost of moving to a smaller railway network system was so vast that even when a later evaluation was carried out of further networks, 7, 8 and 9 and the cash flow over the next ten years evaluated, Sir Richard Marsh, the then Chairman of British Rail, was able to tell John Peyton as Minister of Transport that he saw no prospect for a viable railway of any size, with the caveat that if there was a viable railway it must have been even smaller than some of the already very small railway systems evaluated.

In the meantime, the Second Corporate Plan, covering the years 1973–7, was submitted to the Minister for Transport Industries on 23 February 1972. Although intensive work had been carried out in the interim on the financial evaluation of varying rail networks, basically the strategy for Railways was very similar to the First Corporate Plan. This was hardly surprising as a full evaluation of system and service had not yet been made and a substantial part of Railways opinion was already convinced that the answer did not lie in the 'small railway' concept.

The evaluations of the various sizes of railway networks were available in mid-1972. On the assumptions employed, particularly about the non-escapability of costs and of the expected premature flight of revenue in the event of sizeable closures being announced, they seemed to prove that the solution did not lie in a large-scale reduction of railway size and in no case did they reveal a prospect of viability for any national rail network, the optimum solution merely showing a lessening of support required from government rather than an operating surplus. Top management at B.R.B. was certainly convinced by these results, although the effect on the Department officials was probably more speculative. The method used in evaluation of the various size networks was necessarily a selective one and, in certain civil servants' minds, there was undoubtedly still the lingering suspicion that 'something slightly smaller or slightly different' could perhaps be made viable. Doubt still lingered in the civil servants' minds and yet further studies on 'Viable Railways A and B, with or without lower investment options' were requested, with the not unexpected result that serious planning was hampered by the resources diverted to this work.

It was at this stage that the Board decided to prepare its own review, which later became known as the 'Railway Policy Review'.

This was on a longer time-scale than the previous corporate plans and included strategic reviews involving major considerations of energy, demand and potential, expected population distribution, etc. stretching to the end of the century. It did not offer solutions, but in the inclusion of an interim rail strategy it suggested the direction that would need to be followed in order to meet the major strategic problems assuming a continuing railway.

At a series of meetings with the Minister, Department and Treasury officials, and the executives of the railway unions, the various strategic problems were demonstrated, as was the proposed interim strategy. Basically, these were accepted by the then Minister of Transport, when he said

'In July last year, I told the House of a significant deterioration in British Railways' finances. This led me to conclude that the financial provisions of the 1968 Act, like all previous attempts to solve the railways' difficulties, had proved inadequate and that new legislation would be needed. Since then, the Railways Board has, at my request, in close consultation with my Department, been conducting a series of thorough studies on the prospects and needs of its industry. In considering the conclusions, I have taken account of wider transport policy considerations.

The Board's studies showed no prospect in the foreseeable future of a railway network of anything like the present size being viable. Three possible options were therefore considered against the background of social and economic needs, the preservation of the environment and the conservation of energy supplies. The first is wholesale withdrawal from large areas, achieving savings in the long run, but with high transition costs. The second is piecemeal closure of a significant number of individual loss-making passenger services. The economies would be relatively small, since most of the system costs would remain while revenues fell. The Government do not believe that either of those alternatives would be in the country's interest.

The third and, in the Government's view, the right course, is to maintain a railway network of roughly the present size and to improve it. Unremunerative passenger services should be kept in being as long as they are justified on social and environmental grounds.

The Government broadly accept the strategy recommended by the Railways Board. This will mean substantially high investment in four key areas.'[21]

As we shall see later in this chapter, the ink on this excerpt from Hansard was barely dry before there was a further change in government policy and a reduction in the anticipated level of support.

Following the departure of the Conservative government in 1974, there should have been some comfort for the railways in the announcement, apparently indicating government acceptance, made by Peyton's successor, Fred Mulley, who stated:

'The previous Government, therefore, put in hand a further review with a view to establishing whether there could be a viable railway network at all and what railway system should be provided in the public interest, taking account of social and environmental factors.

This Bill is the outcome and it gives statutory recognition for the first time to the fact that the railways are not a normal nationalised industry but a unique type of public corporation which exists to serve social and environmental purposes as well as the economic needs. I should like to aknowledge the contribution of my predecessor the Rt Hon Member for Yeovil [Mr Peyton], who asked for the review and who, as I understand it, reached a similar conclusion.'[22]

In the meantime the Third Corporate Plan was being processed on the tacit assumption that government acceptance of the interim strategy and its implications would continue and this Third Corporate Plan was submitted to the Minister on 31 January 1975. By that stage it had already become a casualty of one of the inherent difficulties which is always faced in the preparation of a plan for a complex industry. The normal period of gestation for the Board's plans was about nine months and naturally they contained various assumptions about inflation. In the years of the First and Second Corporate Plans, because of the history of comparatively low rates of inflation, a basic tenet had been the assumption that expected incidences of increased costs could be matched by increased prices without any loss of volume and indeed would leave room for the possibility of 'real' price increases in line with the planned improvements of services on both the passenger and freight sides of the business. The annual rate of inflation attained in 1974/75 is now a matter of historic record and this was only too apparent by the time that the Third Corporate Plan was completed.

Whilst it was a comparatively easy matter to adjust indices to provide an arithmetically improved financial evaluation of the plan at the then current rates of inflation, it was not possible in the time to revise the basic strategies which had underlain the development of the specific business/resources plans and, indeed, to do so would have implied that such an expected rate of inflation was to become the norm rather than the exception. However the plan was still submitted as a basis for discussion and with the hope that by joint appraisal with the Department of the Environment help could be obtained in the development of the next corporate plan.

The Fourth Corporate Plan, which covered the years 1976–81 and a snapshot of 1986, was duly prepared but was not adopted either by the Board nor submitted formally to the Minister of Transport. It had been produced as a technical up-date of the strategies inherent in C.P.3 and as such showed the staggering effect of inflation on the Railways' forecast. There had been no time to complete the extensive investigation required on the problems of the freight business which were so savagely accentuated by inflation and the end result was not acceptable to the Board and certainly would not have been financially acceptable to the politicians.

With these difficulties one might ask what course has top Railways management pursued in the absence of overall objectives and, as mentioned previously, in the face of nonacceptance of submitted Corporate Plans? No business can exist in a vacuum as to medium-term intentions and this is particularly true in the case of the Railways business where major investment schemes, e.g. electrification, design of new locomotives or even replacement of existing coaching stock, take from three to five years to come to fruition from initial approval stage. In effect, what has happened is that individual strands which together made up a corporate plan have been pursued. Unfortunately, not all of the strands have been accepted by government or progressed, so that what was initially evaluated has become a political patchwork based on the 'art of the possible'. It could be argued that the very nature of the refusal to follow certain strands by government officials should have given indications to the Railways Board of areas where their plans were being rejected, thus leading to a modified plan. If these rejections had been based on any tenable logic this would indeed have been the case but in reality no detectable pattern has emerged, rejections seeming very often to rely more on temporary political expediency than on any thought out policy.

These were based often on formal powers entrusted to government officials through Acts. Sometimes, however, this was not the case with government relying on their general position or the goodwill of the industry to attain the changes government might be seeking for whatever reasons. Often in these cases government relied on the argument that only it could interpret what was in the national interest. To attempt to achieve this, government has sometimes felt that it was right to reject what might be to the advantage of the industry for the reasons that it might be to the disadvantage of the nation. There are specific instances of government or civil service intervention in various areas with sometimes profound financial effects on the Railways Board's current and future performance. The public evidence is particularly strong in the areas of pricing and investment, and it may be of interest to the reader to consider these items in more detail.

7.1.1 Pricing

With the removal of the requirement to submit a case for fares increases before the Transport Tribunal in the London area following the 1968 Act, the Railways Board in theory should have been free to practise those pricing policies that would help them to match any objectives that are set. However, the proposals by the British Railways Board, made in February 1968, to increase passenger fares and freight charges in 1969 were trapped by the blanket reference arising from the Prime Minister's announcement on 7 September 1967 that all future major price increases in the nationalised industries would be referred to the National Board for Prices and Incomes. That Board reported on the proposals linking them with a reference previously made in October 1967 when the London Area proposals had become entangled with those of London Transport.[23] The Prices and Incomes Board were able to recommend that the application for general increases in standard passenger fares, certain freight traffics and the 'headroom' application up to specified percentages should not be granted whilst allowing percentage increases on scale rates for sundries and parcels and the London Area passenger fares in line with London Transport.

They were apparently able to do this despite the fact that in their report they stated

'The reference requires us to examine the application for fares and charges increases in the light of the financial objective set by the Government for the British Railways Board. The terms in which the objective is expressed are such that we cannot determine precisely what revenue British Rail will need to raise in any one year–and in 1969 in particular–in order to meet it.'[24]

Such is the wisdom of Solomon!!

From 5 July 1971 to September 1972 a 'voluntary' price freeze was imposed on the nationalised industries by the then Chancellor of the Exchequer, Anthony Barber, following agreement with the C.B.I. to limit price increases to a maximum of 5%. This upset the precarious financial balance of the Railways, particularly as at this stage there was no comparable gesture so far as wages were concerned and railway unions were successfully negotiating increases of the order of 10% in 1971 and 13% in 1972.

In November 1972 there was a 114 day complete freeze on pay, prices and dividends under the government's *Counter Inflation (Temporary Provisions) Act 1972*. This prohibited the Railways Board's proposed price increases due to take effect on 1 January 1973. The complete freeze was followed by Stage 2 of the Counter Inflation Policy. The Board was understandably one of the first to make an application to the newly formed Price Commission. Whilst the Board's proposals for fares and charges increases which would have resulted in a weighted average increase of 5.6% were allowable under the provisions of the code relating to nationalised industries, the Minister of the day, Mr John Peyton, intervened with the result that the Board ended up with an increase on passenger fares of some 5% with only a minimal increase in freight and parcels charges. This was to have a profound effect on the economics of the freight business.

In 1974 intervention took place in two ways. The increasing national economic pressures now placed the civil servants in the role of urging the Railways to greater fares increases than those recommended by management, even though it was most forceably argued that the judgement was that larger increases would result in a sharp loss of volume in certain price sensitive areas. It was at this stage that the final remnants of the policy in force since 1968 were swept aside. The previous policy was replaced by an attempt to maximise the revenue, even at the expense of existing or potential volume. This resulted in severe price increases, e.g. 12½% in June, with further price increases recommended for October. There was, of course, a General Election in October 1974 and, in the event, passenger fare increases were postponed until January 1975.

In 1975, with no election and with the country in the grip of an economic recession, approval was given to the following increases:

January	1975	Passenger	12.5%
May	1975	Passenger	15%
September	1975	Passenger	15%

The cumulative effect of these belated attempts to match the gap that had been occurring between passenger revenue and costs was such that savage volume losses were experienced, particularly on the Inter-City services.

7.1.2 Investment

The system of annual investment reviews, coupled with the rolling five-year horizon, is fairly standard procedure in the case of all nationalised industries. In theory it would seem to provide a reasonable basis for medium-term planning, given a measure of agreement and a permanence of the agreed investment figures for an industry. The caveats have, in the case of British Rail, proved to be the factors that have undermined the practical use of the system in force where there has been little measure of agreement and no degree of permanence, even in imposed levels of investment.

To see the importance of this in the strategic railway context one must consider the investment profile of railways since early nationalisation, i.e. 1948. Fig. 7.1. shows this for the years 1948–76 at average 1975 money values. A very significant feature is the high level of investment expenditure in the years 1956–64, the consequence of the implementation of various modernisation plans. However, with a maximum life on moveable assets of twenty to twenty-five years, one would expect to see a repeat of the profile of investment expenditure in the years 1976–85, even if this peak were somewhat lower in size as a result of the contraction in the Railways industry in the intervening years.

Railway management was certainly aware of this high level invest-

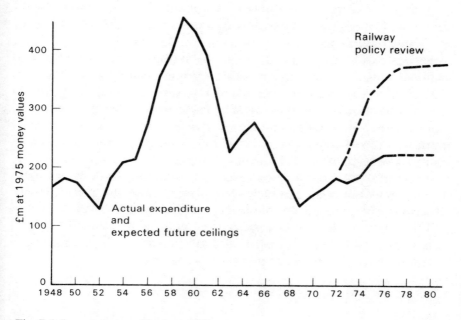

Fig. 7.1 Investment profile since 1948

ment requirement. In the Railway Policy Review prepared during the course of 1973 they included in the expected investment for the years 1974–80, their own estimate of requirement levels.

The force of their arguments was apparently accepted by Mr (now Sir) John Peyton, and in his announcement in November 1973 he indicated an accepted level of investment for the years 1974–80 inclusive. Again national economic pressures intervened and there was almost immediately a reduction in the authorised ceiling for the forthcoming year with the rather optimistic expectation that this could be recovered in the latter years of the cycle. A much lower level of investment was arbitrarily imposed by the government to cover the years 1975–80. This did not provide for any growth in the level of investment and has heavily influenced all subsequent planning activities.

To summarise, in this section we have examined the relationship of British Railways with government in the United Kingdom. This has been a difficult relationship partly because the objectives for the two are different as well as the time-scales that each would wish to work to. Even if there were no problems in these areas, difficulties would probably have arisen because each party has never been clear of what is expected of itself and the other party with respect to certain responsibilities. This may have arisen because formal relationships have not been built on foundations solid enough to survive changes of government or because committees set up by Parliament to investigate British Rail or other nationalised industries have been given little power and authority to remedy what they may have thought to be wrong in the industry or its relationship with government. Whatever the reasons, it is clear that the changing requirements resulting from such instabilities have not been conducive to planning either for the future in British Rail or, indeed, for the health of its financial performance.

However, we live in changing times and, as mentioned earlier, relationships between British Rail and government have improved recently. Further details are provided in chapter 9.

7.2 European government and harmonisation procedures

In Volume 1 of the Consultation Document it is stated that the

> 'E.E.C. has had no major impact in shaping domestic transport policy. In certain areas, however, the common rules existing in the Community and those now under study would have a significant effect on transport operations in this country'.[25]

This section is concerned with exploring some of these issues as they impose in a general way on British Rail but more importantly as they potentially may impose, in a specific way, on corporate and financial planning procedures in British Rail. None of these issues is as yet clear-cut. Whilst it may be clear from the provisions of the Articles of the Treaty of Rome what the ultimate target may be for transport policy in Europe, there are varying interpretations put on their implementation. This relates to many issues but we shall discuss three such issues, namely those that relate to costing procedures, those that surround the question of grants and finally infrastructure costing.

Before discussing these issues in detail, however, it would be useful to note, in summary form, the requirements of the Treaty of Rome and the subsequent legislation as it affects British Rail.

The provisions of Articles 2 and 3 of the Treaty of Rome require the E.E.C. to adopt 'a common policy in the field of transport'. Articles 74–84 relate specifically to the transport sector and lay down certain ground rules including:

(a) the provision that state aids shall be compatible with the Treaty if they meet the needs of transport coordination or are intended as compensation for public service obligations. (Art. 77)

(b) the principle of non-discrimination by carriers on the grounds of the country of origin or destination of goods. (Art. 79)

(c) limitation of transport provisions to road, rail and inland waterways until such time as the Council of Ministers decides unanimously on an extension to sea and air transport. (Art. 84)

In addition to these provisions, there has been broad agreement by the Common Market Governments on the following general principles:

(a) the ultimate achievement of equal conditions of departure in competition among the three modes of inland transport.

(b) non-discrimination against carriers by governments or against customers by transport operators.

Thus, much of the original philosophy was to allow the transport sector to function on the basis of a market economy with the avoidance of artificial distortions, while at the same time making provision for social (including environmental) costs and benefits to be taken into account. In this way, it was hoped that transport would play its proper role in the development of the economy of the Community as a whole, with the achievement of a proper balance among economic, social and environmental objectives.

Much of the subsequent legislation has re-echoed these provisions and principles. This legislation has manifested itself in one of three ways. One of these is in the form of a Decision of the Community, which is concerned only with specific problems within a country and may not be directed to the European Community as a whole. An example of such a Decision is that of 20 May 1975 which relates to the relationships between governments and railways in the Community. Whilst it may be convenient that these relationships should be the same in every Community country, a Decision recognises the unique problems within a country that surround government–railway relationships. Thus the Decision 327 requires 'an improvement of the situation of railways and the harmonisation of rules governing financial relations between railways and states' and may set broad guidelines by which this may be achieved. However, the actual way in which it is achieved is not just left to the parties concerned within the country but to the parties and the Community representatives. Because this is an important piece of Community legislation we shall return to this particular directive.

Because of the heterogeneous nature and organisation of transport undertakings in the Community, it is almost inevitable that much of the legislation is of the Decision kind. But there are two other forms of legislation. A Community Regulation is binding in its entirety and is equivalent to a law. It cannot be changed by the intervention of a national Parliament. An example of a Regulation is 1463/70 of 20 July 1970 which requires the introduction of tachographs to road lorries. The U.K. is in breach of this law because it was required by the Community that this should take effect from 1 January 1975. Finally, there is the Community Directive which is binding as to the result to be achieved but it is left to the individual member state to decide how to achieve the result. As far as transport legislation is concerned, this method does seem to have been used a great deal.

7.2.1. Harmonisation procedures and financial planning

7.2.1.1 *Accounting systems and uniform principles*   We have already noted that there are at least three levels at which Community legislation affects financial planning. One of these relates to accounting systems and uniform principles.

As far as E.E.C. legislation goes, the most pertinent documents relate to the Decision of 20 May 1975. These require that a target date should be set as 1 January 1978 by which time it was expected by the legislators that not only should the accounting systems and annual accounts of the E.E.C. countries be comparable but also that their costing procedures be uniform. By uniform accounting systems is meant a standard presentation of that financial information that is required by the Community. While this has not yet been achieved, it is not felt that it presents a major problem, and it seems likely that a standard form of balance sheet and profit-and-loss account will eventually be prepared, to which figures would be transposed from national accounts, which would continue in their present form. For this reason, it is the requirements of the uniform costing system which we will concentrate on because there is a fundamental difference in the approach of British Rail compared with the other Community countries.

As far as British Rail is concerned, the guiding principle about costing is that costs should be meaningful in a managerial decision-making framework. In practice, and in general, this means that costs are built up from physical facts of the operations and assume that only direct or avoidable costs are relevant in most situations where competitive considerations are of paramount importance. This assumption is not shared by all Community countries. Some do not follow the *synthetic* approach of British Rail but instead use an *analytical* approach. This latter system owes much to the development of cost allocation procedures as used by French and West German railways where all costs (direct and indirect) are allocated.

Although the French system seems to have mathematical elegance, being based on 'ingenious formulae', British Rail feel that this is an inappropriate method of costing as far as the United Kingdom is concerned. This conclusion is based on considerable experience of using both methods and the belief that analytical costing does not provide a valid base for effective commercial decision-making. It must be borne in mind when considering this conclusion that British Rail is concerned with charging 'what the market can bear' and is not interested in a 'cost plus' method of determining prices. Thus, cost analysis, to British Rail, is concerned to decide the worth of traffic. Moreover, British Rail claims to be much more subject to competition with roads than its equivalents in Europe where road traffic seems to be more controlled than in the United Kingdom.

It is clear that British Rail's costing is not in line with that adopted in some other Community countries. As a consequence of this disagreement the E.E.C. has appointed a firm of consultants to investigate the differences and report back to the E.E.C. with recommendations for the future.

7.2.1.2 *Grants* E.E.C. regulations require member states to provide detailed returns on the amount of state aid that they receive.

As far as E.E.C. legislation is concerned, we are interested in three Regulations that were agreed before Britain's entry into the Common

Market. They are *regulations* 1191, 1192 and 1107 agreed in 1969 and 1970. Regulation 1191 refers to the obligations inherent in the concept of a public service and the rules for calculating compensation when such obligations are imposed. This Regulation is often described as that which gives rise to the 'public service obligation' by which railways receive their main grants from their respective governments.

Regulation 1192 identifies the burdens or benefits placed upon or granted to railways which entitle railways to compensation if they can show that, on balance, they are involved in extra cost in comparison with their competitors after taking into account both burdens and benefits. This Regulation has the short title of 'Normalisation of Accounts'.

Finally, Regulation 1107 has the short title of 'Aids For Transport' and lists other circumstances where state aid may be granted for such things as research and development and certain infrastructure expenditure.

As with a great deal of Community legislation, as far as transport seems to be concerned, the principles enunciated are, on face value, acceptable. Concern arises, however, over the processes of changing the principles to working rules and the ways in which individual governments interpret the rules once they have been established. There are a number of examples of this. As far as 'Aids for Transport' are concerned British Rail have advised the Department of Transport that they, British Rail, assume that the state will be reporting under this heading such things as continuing payments under the *1968 Transport Act*. There seems to be dissension between the parties as to whether this is a valid claim under the Directive. The argument is usually centred around whether certain items of expenditure deserve compensation in their own right or whether they fall within the remit of a P.S.O. As far as 'Normalisation of Accounts' is concerned, there seem also to be differences of interpretation and, whilst there is a degree of uniformity for headings, their content may change from country to country.

The greatest debate of these three regulations, however, seems to surround the content of the P.S.O. We will have to examine in more detail what constitutes infrastructure costs, but it is important to note at this stage that, even if it could be assumed that what constituted an infrastructure cost could be agreed, they seem to be treated differently in the U.K. and the Continent. For example, it seems to be standard practice in the U.K. that infrastructure costs largely go straight to revenue account. On the Continent, standard practice on the other hand, seems to be to charge infrastructure costs to capital account, even for renewal items.

7.2.1.3 *Infrastructure costs* Legislation about infrastructure costs goes back to early 1966 and has been the subject of academic research, debate and controversy for the majority of the period between 1966 and 1979. The nature of the research, debate and controversy surrounds three issues. The first and least important of these is concerned with what physical things are to be included in infrastructure costs. An example of this is the different approach taken in the U.K. from that on the Continent to fences around railways; in the U.K. this is an obligatory requirement but not on the Continent. The questions such requirements pose relate to how comparable any figures are even in accounts that are supposed to be normalised.

More important issues have been raised about the non-physical side of infrastructure costs; that is, those costs that are associated 'social', 'environmental' and other 'external' costs. Most of the E.E.C. recommendations in this area have been based on theoretical works in economics. In general, work in this area assumes that infrastructure charges to users should be based on marginal *social* cost, and not just marginal cost as advocated by Cmnd 3437. Moreover, it is also assumed that if the sum total of revenue based on these marginal social costs failed to cover total expenditure on infrastructure, then there would be a system of balancing tolls to ensure budget equilibrium.

As we have already noted this may be a perfectly acceptable 'in principle' philosophy to attempt to follow. But this is a more difficult philosophy to put into practice than most of the other principles that we have noted because economic theory has not developed a mechanism, acceptable to all economic theorists, by which social costs may be calculated or balancing tolls may be allocated among services so as to achieve budget equilibrium. However, a considerable amount of theoretical work has been done in this field and some of it, for example, recommends that balancing tolls should be proportional to marginal social costs.[26] This proposal was put forward on the grounds that users should pay directly for the benefits they derived from an 'over large' infrastructure. By 'over large' is meant an infrastructure that is larger than is justified simply and strictly on economic grounds. The calculation of the social benefits that justify the 'over large' infrastructure involves not only calculations that involve rail directly but also other modes of transport. For example, they could involve, at least on a conceptual level, the benefits to be derived from keeping traffic off roads and the resulting savings in accidents and pollution. This inter-modal calculation of social costs and benefits is extremely difficult to undertake. Even for one transport mode, Gwilliam *et al* considered–in an unpublished report to the Commission–that there would be considerable difficulties in linking the concept of marginal social cost pricing to investment in urban areas although this was not necessarily true of inter-urban situations.[27]

Even if there were general agreement on a conceptual level, there would be considerable problems attached to the practical application of a marginal social cost pricing rule. There are significant conceptual and practical difficulties associated with a marginal cost pricing rule but the position about social costs and other 'external' costs is very much more complicated. There is first a problem of identifying the so called 'external' factors. Whilst one may agree that they may have something to do with things such as pollution and accidents, it is much more difficult to identify the precise nature of pollution and accidents. Then, there is the age old problem of quantifying the effects of such things as pollution and accidents.

The most contentious issue about infrastructure costs, however, seems to relate to effects they have between different modes of traffic. In essence much of the argument relates to the fact that rail users have to pay for track costs directly while road users only pay for roads indirectly. It is further argued that, in the freight field, this gives an unfair advantage to lorries because they are not required to pay an adequate amount for the use they make of roads; in other words the car may subsidise the lorry. As far as British Rail is concerned, it has argued that it wishes to have an infrastructure grant so that it could compete on a fairer basis. This has been rejected by the state largely on the basis that it would infringe E.E.C. regulations, a finding which British Rail rejects.

We noted earlier in this section that there is broad agreement with the principle that there should be equal conditions of departure for competition among modes of transport. This is nearer the case in Europe than it seems to be in the U.K., a situation that the Consultation Document seems to concede, in that it recognises the need for adjustment in terms of competition among modes, or an overlay of physical constraints.[28] However, British Rail contends in its reply that the recognised adjustment still 'stops well short of current E.E.C. regulations and requirements on *road* transport. If these were implemented *in toto* the "price inelastic" nature of road freight demand could come under very severe strain indeed'.[29]

7.2.2 Business planning

One of the most important Decisions made by the Council, as far as financial planning is concerned, is that made on 20 May 1975, that is Decision 327. Within the articles of this Decision a number of requirements are set out. We have already noted that under Article 8.2 the Council shall, before 1 January 1978, adopt the necessary measures to achieve comparability among accounting systems and lay down uniform costing principles, and that these could affect the way that financial planning is carried out.

Articles 3, 4, 5, 13 and 14 are much more specific about planning. Article 3 requires, for example, that each railway undertaking shall 'submit its business plans, possibly covering a number of years, including its investment and financing programmes within the framework of overall policies laid down by the State and taking account of national transport planning, particularly with regard to infrastructure'.

Article 4 states, among other things, that the business plan 'be settled in the context of a procedure decided by the state and based on consultation between the state and the undertaking. The plan shall be drawn up with the aim of achieving financial balance for the undertaking as well as other technical, commercial and financial management objectives. The plan shall also lay down the method of implementation'. Article 4 also requires that the state monitor the implementation of the plan and determine the public service order obligations to be met by railway undertakings.

Article 5 refers to the ways by which the state and the railway undertaking will settle procedures that relate to repayments, consolidations and conversion of loans and the respective proportions in which new investments may be financed from internal sources, by borrowing or by direct state grants. It also stresses that capital grants must be intended to increase the assets of the railway undertaking.

Article 13 states that 'In conjunction with the railway undertaking, the state shall draw up a financial programme aimed at achieving the financial balance of the undertaking. Under this programme, the state may grant to the railway, deficit subsidies which must be distinct.' This goes on to enumerate these, of which the most important are the public service obligations.

Finally, Article 14 stresses that every two years the commission should submit to the Council a report on Decision 327 as well as Regulations 1191, 1192 and 1107. It further stresses that this report should clearly indicate the results achieved with particular emphasis on the financial situation of the railways undertakings.

We have quoted a lot from Decision 327 because of its importance to the financial planning procedures. The requirements of the Decision are not 'pie in the sky' suggestions, for this is a Decision implementable from 1 January 1977 and many of its requirements came into force on the equivalent day in 1978.

Some of the implications of the requirements are reasonably clear with respect to financial planning and ought to be highlighted before this section is concluded. For example, it seems reasonably clear that business plans become a necessary obligation rather than something the railways might undertake just out of interest. The overall content of the plan is also specified in broad principle terms. Furthermore, it seems equally clear that deficit financing is not allowed under this Decision and, finally, the stressing of progress report shows the clear intention of the Council to monitor the plans.

There are other issues however that are not so clear in the wording of the Decision and further clarification will have to be sought on these. For example, Article 4 seems to place emphasis on the state judging the merits or demerits of the plan. If we are to comment on the basis of the evidence found in the N.E.D.O. report on nationalised industries in the U.K., it might be argued that this would be an inappropriate procedure, because of different time-scales and objectives held by the two parties concerned.

Article 4 uses the words 'financial balance' without defining the meaning of this. Does it, for example, mean 'breaking even' or is some other definition to be used? Is the definition to be used to be the same for each community country? Similarly Article 5 uses general statements about the state and the railway undertakings 'settling procedures' relating to repayments, consolidations, etc. Whilst it is clear that capital grants have to increase the assets of the railway undertakings, no appropriate procedures are suggested for the state–industry debate.

Finally Article 13 seems to emphasise that the state takes the initiative in drawing up a financial programme aimed at achieving the financial balance of the undertaking. Again, it seems, from British evidence at least, that it is difficult to reconcile the different time-scale and objectives of the state and nationalised industries.

7.3 Summary

The foregoing chapter will have served to give some indication of the problems facing corporate and financial planners in British Rail. The variations in statutory policy have certainly presented an ever changing scene to those involved in determining forward strategy. Whether this will be clarified or further complicated by the legislation on transport policy going through Parliament in 1980 remains to be seen.

The emergence of corporate planning in the early 1970s and the reception accorded to the early plans may well serve to give an indication of the poor relationships between the Railways Board and the Department of Transport. This must surely have been the almost inevitable consequence of increased information being rendered ineffective because of the absence of an overall objective.

The intervention of government in such matters as pricing, investment and level of support can be described as the short-term tinkerings in the absence of an agreed objective. Difficulties are further heightened by the E.E.C. attempts to introduce a uniform approach to transport problems in the member states. Dare one suggest that, until we have assigned a national role to railways, it will be impossible for the U.K. to do more than pay lip service to the Commission's approach or even to play its proper part in the determination of such an approach.

Cynically, one might come to the conclusion that corporate and financial planning under such circumstances is a waste of time in the absence of certain of the basic inputs to any form of corporate planning. However, there is no doubt that, within the Railways, the production of the series of corporate plans mentioned previously, even though they have not been carried through to their logical conclusion of action plans etc., has certainly served to clarify the minds of management, planners and government about the basic facts of the business. One can only hope that by learning from the mistakes of the past not only planning but the strategic importance of the railways in the national scene will be fully recognised by both sides.

As far as the E.E.C. is concerned, nothing major has been achieved on shaping domestic transport policy but this seems unlikely to remain the case. The major effect on financial planning in British Rail may be in changing accounting procedures, costing procedures in the way grants are allocated from the state and how government may be involved in planning. All of these would be fundamental changes. There is, however, the possibility that changes may go further than this. For example, if the E.E.C. intends to try to put into practice the principle of 'equal conditions of departure of competition between modes' it may use the calculations of infrastructure costs as one means of attempting to do this, and this could give rise to considerable problems of a conceptual nature, as well as practical problems in financial planning.

EIGHT

Issues in Financial Planning as Exemplified in British Rail

Financial planning, like most complex activities, is still developing both at the process and at the mechanisms level. This is not merely because of the introduction of computerised figure manipulation but because a greater understanding of the subject is being accumulated, leading to conceptual developments and responses to changing needs. This chapter will consider some of these issues, using British Rail as a case study. In doing so, we will touch on some matters which are vital to British Rail's financial planning, which will be covered in greater detail in chapter 9.

8.1 Financial planning and corporate planning

The relationship between these two processes has been described in chapter 2, where the role of financial planning has been significantly elevated beyond a level which many corporate planners or, indeed, accountants would accept. We feel that chapter 2 creates the right perspective but raises the question, how could a less significant role for financial planning have been established in recent years?

Part of the reason for this must lie in the part played by accountants who have been slow to react to changing circumstances. Their traditional financial accounting/auditing roles gradually gave way to a management accounting role in the 1960s, although considerable activity in developing costing procedures took place before that period. However, the management accounting role did not develop quickly enough to enable accountants to prepare financial plans of the nature indicated in chapter 2. Instead, effort was concentrated on investment appraisal techniques (D.C.F. was quite a surprise to many well established accountants), budgetary control (revenue and capital budgets) and the development of more adequate costing techniques involving incremental and avoidable costs. The net result of this was that when corporate planning was 'imported' from America, it was regarded as a new science but its logical financial planning element had yet to be properly developed.

Many organisations set up corporate planning departments to tackle the production of their corporate plans. Others placed the responsibility on their accounting departments, presumably recognising a strong financial bias. Management accountants in these organ-isations suddenly inherited a broader responsibility which, in many cases, they were forced to share with others as part of a small corporate planning department, often employing business school graduates as analysts and as general planners as well as the usual specialists. The development of broader financial planning was, therefore, swallowed-up in the implementation and development of corporate planning. The irony of this situation is the fact that most of these organisations established only financial objectives and, in our view, have only been tackling financial planning.

It is a matter of concern that the accountancy profession can be considered to have been too slow to react (let alone proact) to developments in the business world. Also, it will be unfortunate if a rift is established between corporate planning departments and finance departments in organisations. This will be particularly likely where the corporate plans identify financial objectives only. A measure of such friction existed in British Rail in the early 1970s but has been overcome.

What then of the future for financial planning as part of corporate planning? The answer lies partly in the development of financial planning techniques and model-building (again mostly for financial planning) but also in the development of corporate planning itself. Financial planning and modelling will be discussed in later sections. Let us now confine our discussions to the likely future developments of corporate planning. The sophistication of the corporate planning procedures is likely to be patchy when compared with the outline theory given in chapter 2. This will reflect the culture and structure of the organisations which will influence their values, and lead to varying potentiality and propensity for change. For this reason corporate planning will not tend to equalise competing organisations. It is more likely to assist the strong and ambitious at the expense of the weak and unsure.

What will probably not be achieved within the next ten years, however, is a considerable expansion of the establishment of non-financial objectives. Thus, many corporate plans will continue to be financial plans with an incorrect title. The reasons for this include such things as the attitude that all other areas of ambition are of secondary importance, to be relegated to the role of constraints upon the financial objective, and the difficulty of deciding upon clear-cut and acceptable objectives in employment and establishing social responsibilities. Thus, in the guise of and as part of corporate planning, we expect major developments in the establishment of overall financial planning routines within the next ten years. Coupled with procedural developments which will be discussed later, the next ten-year period will be as vital as the last ten have proved to be. It is to be hoped that the accountancy profession will respond to the challenge.

8.2 Financial planning issues–general

Within companies in the private sector, the determination of financial objectives has usually been kept to a fairly simple concept of a required return on investment, return on capital employed or absolute profit before tax. These would seem to be fully appropriate and capable of being used in modified form as an overall measure and as sub-objectives for sectors of the business. Problems arise, however, in translating such procedures into a form suitable for use in the nationalised industries and the rest of the public sector.

Looking first at the nationalised industries, it must be said that it should be possible to use such criteria as return on investment or return on capital employed. However, many would find this rather difficult because the nationalised industries have not always been run on fully commercial bases, at the behest of government. The British Rail example is perhaps the most extreme, but it does serve to illustrate the problem. With British Rail having to perform a social service in some aspects of its business, at a considerable loss, having experienced price controls beyond its wishes and having received the benefits of succesive capital write-offs to reduce its losses and indebtedness, a return to such criteria is hardly appropriate. One could, however, devise such a system for the non-passenger side of the Railways business and the non-railway businesses, given that a realistic figure for total investment or capital employed could be agreed with the Department of Transport.

However, since 1976 the government has chosen to deal with absolute levels of cash transfer and of investment as being the main measures of success, i.e. as the financial objectives, although some of the nationalised industries have been or are still required to work to varying percentage returns on capital employed. In the case of British Rail, the objective has been to break even one year with another, now after receipt of government payments. Since 1973 however this process has been completely overtaken by inflation and the situation is overdue for review. In these years, losses and grants in the nationalised industries have become the rule rather than the exception. This was a major influence on the introduction of cash limits in 1976, and has been coupled with increases in local authority and central government spending, particularly between 1973 and 1975, and led to the impression, in many quarters, that government expenditure was out of control. Thus, some of the nationalised industries are now faced with a new situation—cash limits on grants and deficits and on investment. As we saw in chapter 5, within British Rail this situation manifests itself in the shape of the P.S.O. cash limit, the non-passenger deficit cash limit and the investment 'ceiling' cash limit which has the unfortunate difficulty of including investment classed as revenue which is also contained within the other cash limits. More recently, British Rail has started working to a financing cash limit as well.

If all the nationalised industries were to become profitable within the next few years, then the cash limit procedure would become largely invalid and profit objectives more relevant. However, this assumes the elimination of grants, which is not very likely, nor is the speedy elimination of losses in some organisations, e.g. British Steel Corporation. Instead, it would appear that the cash limit procedures will become increasingly important as a means of government control over some of the nationalised industries in all four aspects: grants, deficits, investment and overall financing. What must be considered, therefore, is what criteria of acceptability will be established.

Before considering this point, however, it should be noted that the cash limit procedure has become a major feature of the existence of the rest of the public sector. Prior to 1976, the call on the public purse was according to demonstrated need. Now the arrangements are more arbitrary and this has had a major effect on the development proposals of other non-profit making organisations in the public sector such as local authorities and the health service. Here again the question of acceptable levels of cash limit needs to be considered, linked to acceptable measures of output where they can be established.

To date, the method of determining the levels of individual cash limits has been arbitrary. Distributing the agony on a more-or-less *pro rata* basis seems to have become the new rule in place of demonstrated need. We have seen that, in the case of British Rail, the P.S.O. cash limit has been fixed according to the 1975 level, plus an allowance for inflation. The same situation has applied to the level crossing grant and the investment 'ceiling', and the freight and parcels deficit subsidy cash limit had been scaled down to nil by January 1978. These arrangements are fairly typical of those now applied in the public sector where any form of public purse cash transfer is required from central government.

No proper criterion of acceptability seems yet to have been established for the levels of cash limits. However, the procedure should not be under-rated. Indeed, many would argue that it is a major step in the right direction in controlling public expenditure. Further, in terms of reducing public expenditure in real terms, it can be claimed to be a success, the trend of outlay having been halted and even reversed. However, other circumstances have worked in favour of the cash limits procedure in the shape of controls on wages. The national pay policy phases 1 and 2 pay increases were substantially below the general level of inflation, and the public bodies, by and large, did not allow wages drift through other causes to undermine its benefit. Consequently, the cash limit procedure can be said to be not fully tested: its acid test will not arise until freedom in wage bargaining is fully established. Within British Rail it is evident that the P.S.O. cash limit in 1976 and 1977 would have been exceeded had the annual pay settlement been of the order of the level of inflation or, as would perhaps be required by the unions, two or three percentage points above the retail prices index.

Be that as it may, the cash limits procedure has proved that a way can be found for government to exercise a decisive influence on affairs in the public sector. It has produced a situation which is a little more akin to that in the private sector, which depends for its survival on working within an even more stringent financial framework which requires regular demonstrations of solvency and performance, and an atmosphere of confidence about future expectations. It would be unrealistic to think that the public sector, or even its nationalised industries, could ever emulate the private sector completely. That would require a considerable reduction in government influence in favour of market influences. However, it is quite likely that the cash limits procedure will eventually be taken further in the shape of more flexibility in the setting of limits and the creation of profit objectives, where the grant situation does not apply.

Despite the difficulties associated with the determination of a return on investment or return on capital employed within the nationalised industries, there are signs that the Treasury would like to do this, where profit targets seem appropriate, rather than cash limits, e.g. the railways freight business. A real return of 5% on capital employed has been mooted and the concept discussed in Cmnd 7131.[1] Apart from the difficulties of establishing the capital side of the equation, it is unlikely that the nationalised industries could meet such a requirement in the short term. This would require results which are considerably better than those obtained in recent years. If such a system is adopted to determine flexible cash limits and profit objectives (where appropriate) for the nationalised industries, then it is strongly recommended that the capital side of the equation be the subject of a special reassessment in most cases. This should take care of the unrealistic balance sheet values which currently exist and substitute more suitable post-depreciation figures. The criteria laid down in Exposure Draft 24 for current cost accounting (C.C.A.), which is covered in section 8.3.2, would presumably form the basis of such assessments. However, it must be recognised that if depreciation is charged to the accounts on a C.C.A. basis also, as should be the case shortly, then the 5% requirement, covering profits after depreciation, begins to look more realistic, even if difficult.

It will be interesting to see how the cash limits procedures develop in the next few years within the public sector. It is not unreasonable to postulate that they will remain in force for a long time and that the determination of their levels will remain somewhat arbitrary but with a slight swing towards discrete assessments based on required return on capital employed or on demonstrated need, as circumstances dictate. Many of the circumstances are likely to be emergencies. As far as British Rail is concerned, the arbitrary nature of the procedure is likely to remain until pay settlements or general economic conditions create results that severely test the cash limits. This could be sooner, rather than later.

Related to the issue of cash limits for nationalised industries is the question of how they are capitalised. By and large capital funds are provided to the nationalised industries by way of long-term loans, either from central government or with central government backing. There are two exceptions to the rule, British Airways and the British Steel Corporation. In both of these instances the financing arrangements allow for a measure of equity capital as well as long-term loans. The argument goes that this is necessary because both organisations are trading internationally and should not be placed in a potentially disadvantageous position in terms of costs. This rather pre-supposes that the dividend level might, on some occasions at least, need to be lower than the cost of loan capital. Such equity capital is known as public dividend capital recognising government ownership and perhaps the evocative nature of the term share capital which does not comply with a nationalised industry image.

There has been some debate on the case for a considerable extension of this process to a degree perhaps which covers about two-thirds of the long-term capitalisation of all nationalised industries.[2] The existing situation heavily penalises the nationalised industries in times when the national economic situation is depressed. This problem may be coupled with the fact that there seems to be an unwritten law that nationalised industries should not make large profits since this would display capitalist tendencies. As a consequence, they incur huge borrowings to finance investment which is inadequately covered by the low profits they are allowed to earn and low depreciation they are allowed to charge on a historical basis. This results in escalating interest charges and, in some cases (British Rail being the prime example), to capital reconstructions to prevent the interest being so large as to be farcical. To a large extent, inflation accounting will cure this problem because 'true' profits and losses will become available. This will almost certainly lead to price increases, where these are practical, to cover very large increases in depreciation which convert small profits into large losses. This will not remove the intellectual justification for a measure of equity capital. The nationalised industries are not in complete monopoly situations whether or not they trade internationally. Many compete with each other and most, in some part or form, compete with private industry. It is only reasonable that they be placed on the same footing and be able to pay dividends according to their profit situations, good or bad, rather than interest on long-term loans, most of which will grow until write-offs arise. It is not really anticipated that much action will take place in this area in the next few years but it is hoped that the subject will benefit from continued debate for later action. British Rail have tried to keep the debate open but without much effect.[3]

8.3 Financial planning issues–procedural

Within the total ambit of the financial planning process outlined in chapters 2 and 3, there are a number of procedural developments which require comment. We have selected for discussion those topics that we consider likely to be the most important in the medium-term future.

8.3.1 Computer models

Probably the most important development in the next ten years in financial planning procedures will be the further development of the computer models mentioned in chapter 2, to deal with the figure work involved. We have seen that a major problem which exists at the moment is the fact that it can take many months for an organisation to prepare what we have described as an outline plan (see fig. 2.2) and much longer to develop options to improve the forecast results. The same applies to the action plan stage but not often perhaps to the strategy stage, where the forecasting and evaluation procedures are not usually so detailed. Computer modelling of established financial planning procedures is the logical cure to this problem and will enable more options to be considered within the outline plans and action plan stages within considerably shorter time-scales. This will often have a spin-off effect on the development of strategy because aspects of the strategy, sometimes described as sub-strategic options, can be dealt with by running the outline plan procedure with estimates of the required effect being fed into the evaluation procedures in the detail normally required for the outline plan.

The processes which would be best modelled in respect of the outline plans stage relate to the modular procedures outlined in fig. 2.3 which gives a structured approach to the preparation and use of the separate specifications required to precede the financial evaluations. These procedures are eminently suitable for a modular approach, enabling each department to feel in control of its own patch and make a contribution similar to that which would have applied under manual arrangements. This aspect should not be underestimated because financial planning must be a fully integrated procedure which requires the whole-hearted involvement of all departments within an organisation.

The computer modelling processes, apart from following the established manual procedures can, of course, produce the same level of output, usually in the form of forecast profit-and-loss results and cash flows with supporting physical facts. By the same token, the arrangements could be adapted to fit any requirement for producing a non-financial primary output, rather than supporting data, if that were to be required. In this way, the computer modelling procedures can be used for all aspects of corporate planning and not just financial planning. We expect most large organisations to utilise such computer procedures for aspects of their financial planning during the next ten years. This will be the only way of coping with the complexity of a sophisticated procedure within a reasonable time-scale. British Rail are likely to be near to the forefront of these developments with the whole of their outline plan production being scheduled for computerisation within the next two years.

8.3.2 Inflation accounting

For most of the 1970s the accountancy profession has been considering the need for, and predicted effect of, a form of inflation accounting to replace historical cost accounting, which is clearly out of date in these inflationary times. By and large, the argument has centred upon the desire for current purchasing power (C.P.P.) figures prepared as an adjunct to the historical cost based figures, or for current cost accounting (C.C.A.) which produces figures in current cost terms with the possible elimination of the need for historical cost based figures.

In the event, the Accounting Standards Committee has recently produced a proposal which deals with the various difficulties with a reasonable chance of success.[4] Known as Exposure Draft 24 and coupled with a set of guidance notes, the proposal is to create a form of current cost accounting which is to be undertaken from 1980, in connection with the annual accounts of all listed companies and other organisations with an annual turnover of £5 m or more. However, the current cost profit-and-loss account and the related balance sheet figures are now proposed to be supplementary to the present historical cost based figures.

Briefly the proposal is to produce supplementary statements to the annual accounts which will establish the current cost operating profit, i.e. after making C.C.A. adjustments to the historical depreciation figures, cost of sales adjustments and monetary working capital adjustments, all designed to identify the effect of changing prices. Additionally, it is proposed that a gearing adjustment be calculated to establish the current cost profit attributable to shareholders. Coupled with this will be the current cost balance sheet, wherein fixed assets and stocks would generally be included at their value to the business. This would normally mean net current replacement cost but could be net realisable value or even economic value (opportunity cost) where considered appropriate.

In due course the C.C.A. procedures should create for the nationalised industries a situation whereby it is reasonable to create financial objectives in respect of a return on investment or on capital employed. As mentioned earlier, this is not presently appropriate for many organisations (particularly the nationalised industries), mainly because of unrealistic asset/depreciation figures. Naturally, in the long run, financial planning procedures will also need to be on a compatible basis but this is likely to take a few years to evolve. Much will depend on the perceived success of the C.C.A. accounts and the development of related objectives. However, we feel certain that there is much to be gained from the development of C.C.A. and consider that Exposure Draft 24 is a major milestone.

In dealing with inflation accounting on the C.C.A. basis, British Rail will be in some difficulty in determining their fixed asset values. This applies to operational land and buildings where the net current replacement cost is difficult to assess and to all fixed assets if the opportunity cost approach is used. What, for example, is the opportunity cost value of a fleet of locomotives in a loss-making business? However these problems are overcome, it is interesting to note that the total depreciation charge could increase by as much as £100 m per annum. The effect of this change could be very significant. For example the P.S.O. grant, which allows for depreciation, would perhaps be inflated to a level which more or less finances the investment of the passenger business, eliminating the need for borrowing and the consequent interest burden. One assumes that, in these circumstances, the cash limit would be modified. On the freight and parcels side the higher depreciation would render that combined business as being incapable of breaking even (as presently required), probably for a few years. However, these changes would at least be more realistic, a term which cannot be applied to the current depreciation charges, which have benefited from capital reconstructions. Similar problems exist with the other nationalised industries, including the need for a decision on the usefulness of the gearing adjustment in their circumstances.

8.3.3 Risk and sensitivity analysis

Associated with this development is the growing use of risk and sensitivity analysis, which in many ways can be a great help in financial planning by increasing the understanding of the nature of the forecasts and the extent of their reliability. It is anticipated that these analysis procedures will become more extensively used in the next few years, particularly in regard to outline plans. The risk procedures will require the determination of a large number of probability distributions concerning the input data of the outline plans and the use of 'Monte-Carlo' simulation (requiring a computer, normally) to process them in a useful form. This development will also facilitate improved measurement of the return on capital investment projects. Most of such project evaluations would benefit from such an appraisal. These comments are not meant to minimise the difficulty of assessing probability distributions but to recognise at least that considerable progress must be made in this area if financial planning itself is to progress.

In any part of the financial planning process requiring forecasts, a large element of judgement is involved and the net result is that the 'most likely' outcome is predicted. The overall result in producing the outline plan in this way is that these 'most likely' situations are added together to produce what is considered to be the overall 'most likely' forecast. Quite obviously, each constituent figure could be better or worse by large or small amounts. Indeed, the net result is not likely to be the 'true most likely' unless each constituent forecast is located at the mid-point of a normal frequency distribution.

Organisations having introduced complex corporate and financial planning procedures are now looking at this problem as a major hurdle to be overcome within the next few years. They will produce the sort of risk and sensitivity analyses which suit their perceived needs, ranging from a gross estimate of ranges to a statistical approach to a simulation approach. For their outline plan, British Rail having tried broad ranges (a form of sensitivity analysis) have recently tried a statistical approach through summing *beta* distributions applied to large tranches of receipts and expenditure.[5] This approach has proved very successful because it pointed out the 'most likely' overall forecast is not the 'true most likely' by a significant amount. They are considering taking this analysis much further by designing a simulation model which will deal with a much larger number of elements, each in a discrete fashion through separate probability distributions. A test has been completed using the data from the statistical approach and this has confirmed (and slightly increased) the level of the forecasting error which had been discovered.

It is anticipated that the computer agencies will be geared to cope with these developments as extensions to their financial planning packages. To date, their main forte has been the ability to quickly re-process forecast data to answer the 'what if' type of question. This is absolutely invaluable and will deal with changing planning assumptions, if not sub-strategic options. However, this procedure will not identify the risks attached to the final plan which may require a simulation procedure if it is to be tackled thoroughly.

8.3.4 Investment appraisal

The D.C.F. procedure is now extensively used, and few changes are likely to arise in the central aspect of the process. Instead, it seems likely that most emphasis will be placed on measurement of risk to qualify the forecasts which are being used. The process by which risk has been allowed for in the discount rate is clearly out of date, but it seems unlikely that organisations will move away from their somewhat arbitrary cut-off rates in favour of a more sophisticated evaluation of the cost of capital for each project. Instead, what is likely is that more and more they will construct risk and sensitivity analyses around their 'central' forecasts to aid the decision-making process. This process will be similar to that covered in section 8.3.3 (i.e. simulation) about broader planning forecasts.

This revision will be extremely useful, in that the identification of the risk profile might change the ranking of projects and will certainly sharpen the forecasting process. Also, it might help to identify responsibility where a project vetting process takes place. In these circumstances, the vetting authority must take responsibility because they have considered the risks, the previous absence of which tended to make them 'delegate' responsibility to the project submission level, where it has perhaps been assumed that risks had been taken into account. The importance of this development cannot be understated because it will help compensate for the fact that forecasts used in the D.C.F. investment appraisal process are usually biased. The very nature of the task tends to produce optimistic forecasts to justify the investment. The so-called 'most likely' cash inflows and outflows will often be found to contain what might be described as a systematic error if a thorough risk analysis is undertaken.

Within the nationalised industries the most important development in this area is likely to be the effect of the 1978 White Paper on The Nationalised Industries.[6] This document recognised the fact that the D.C.F. test discount rate procedure has not been fully implemented within the nationalised industries. This results from the fact that much of the investment is for essential replacement of worn-out assets. The proposal is for an overall rate of 5% to be used, to be known as the required rate of return. This rate is to be achieved in real terms for the aggregate incremental return on all of the investment recorded in each corporate plan. An associated accounting rate of return is postulated also for measurement of profit targets as mentioned earlier. This required rate of return of 5% is to be used by all nationalised industries for investment in parts of their organisation not judged to have a social connotation. This would apply to British Rail's freight and parcels business but not to the bulk of the passenger business (perhaps the Inter-city sector would qualify). Lower rates of return might apply to the social areas with a nil return being likely. The White Paper recommends that each nationalised industry might retain the test discount rate as an internal mechanism for ranking projects but the discount rate will not be determined by government. British Rail has chosen to use 7%. These revised rules will be applied from 1979 for overall investment appraisal but not for a measure of overall profit target measurement. This latter aspect will not be sufficiently developed for a number of years.

8.3.5 Other

No doubt in the next few years there will be developments in the areas of budgeting and costing but these are not likely to be fundamental. On the budgeting side the use of profit centres will become even more extensive than now and the use of computer models to help calculate the budgets and monitor the results will be even more so. On the costing side, however, the gradual recognition of the usefulness of profit 'contributions' rather than so called 'profits' after distribution of joint costs is likely to become more intensive and lead to improved procedures.

NINE

Issues in Financial Planning in British Rail

This chapter will consider a number of key and topical issues concerning British Rail's financial planning and future development. We will concentrate mainly on the Railways business, not just because it is the largest within British Rail but because it is receiving most attention in a strategic sense. The chapter deals first with objectives and then with matters of a strategic nature. Some financial planning procedural issues will arise again where they are crucial to the arguments, but this will be kept to a minimum.

9.1 British Rail objectives

The 1977 White Paper on Transport Policy attempted to move towards a co-ordinated transport policy which, as was noted in chapter 7, has been a long-standing ambition of many people. It falls considerably short of that rather grand and highly questionable target. Moreover, the Paper itself recognises that even if full integration were an acceptable target, it could not be attained without careful and considerable discussion by all parties concerned. To this end, the government proposes to publish White Papers on transport policy at intervals of approximately three years which will facilitate that discussion.[1] Thus, the 1977 White Paper must be seen as a stepping stone towards providing the sort of transport system that Britain needs and wants, at the price it can afford. As far as British Rail and financial planning are concerned, the concentration is on setting and meeting medium-term financial targets. This approach is further reinforced by some of the considerations expressed in the 1978 White Paper on nationalised industries.[2] However, the bulk of this chapter will be devoted to a discussion of the 1977 White Paper on transport policy.

This White Paper has yet to be converted into legislation but such legislation seems unlikely to change the statutory requirement for British Rail having to break even subject to grants payable in respect of the Railway passenger business (P.S.O.), P.T.E.s and a grant for certain level crossings expenditure. Also, the further requirements introduced in recent years should not alter significantly, i.e. that the P.S.O. will not exceed a cash limit. The temporary railway freight and parcels grant ceased in 1978, and the overlays concerning the level of investment, fixed to an annual 'ceiling' level, will remain flat in real terms at least up to 1980. The White Paper does not change the fact that the revenue investment part of the investment 'ceiling' cash limit has to be charged to working expenses. This remains, therefore, a complicated procedure because most of the funds involved are also included in the P.S.O. arrangements. The issue of the fiscal year financing cash limit, described in chapter 5, remains to be tackled, however, and could cause considerable problems. Much will depend upon the negotiations taking place on the level of the 1980/81 financing limit, rather than on impending legislation.

Despite not making changes at the conceptual level the White Paper makes considerable use of the cash limits procedure and seeks to formalise and extend the arrangements. Since early 1976, when the government decided that greater effort should be put into control of expenditure, cash limits of varying kinds have become the vogue and, in many cases, have converted loose general objectives into more concrete requirements. This is partly true in respect of British Rail where the Railway P.S.O. cash limits and the freight and parcels deficit cash limits have been regarded as firm and positive targets since 1976, which had to be achieved by whatever means. Indeed, on the evidence of the British Rail situation, the cash limits procedure is a considerable step forward in the identification of financial objectives. The financial objectives created by the *Railways Act 1974*, varying the grants situation created by the *Transport Act 1968*, did little to specify the level of the P.S.O. grant other than to set the maximum amount which could be drawn over an unspecified number of years. The break-even one year with another situation on the freight and parcels side is a little vague in terms of what 'one year with another' means precisely but is a little more positive in that it has been regarded in practice as a break-even every year requirement.

Apart from formalising these arrangements, the 1977 White Paper seeks to make two changes. The first is the imposition of an arbitrary cut of £20 m in 1976 'survey' prices (about £25 m in average 1978 prices) in the P.S.O. cash limit by the end of the decade.[3] This is now understood to mean by the end of the fiscal year 1980/81. The second is the suggestion now operating that the passenger rolling stock replacement programme presently funded by government loans would instead be funded by a special grant, which together with the existing depreciation provision and presumably scrap sales, would be sufficient for that purpose.[4] The purpose of this is to ameliorate the growing P.S.O. interest burden, which would otherwise grow at a considerable rate as there is no facility for repayment of the loans, and as a step towards C.C.A. The annual grant will amount to £50 m in 1978 average prices. This will amount to only two-thirds of the annual requirement to prevent borrowings. This difference is mainly occasioned by the need to invest in stations and other infrastructure items treated as capital investment.

Given these two significant changes, the 1977 White Paper makes a number of further important points which we should consider. On investment, it makes a commitment to the need for a rolling programme to provide for a medium-term security of funds and acceptance of projects.[5] This meets the long-standing British Rail complaint that it cannot plan its investment properly without such a commitment, the absence of which has, in recent years, been expensive in terms of certain investment projects being more costly than they need have been. However, the White Paper does not suggest that the investment 'ceilings' will be allowed to expand, irrespective of the new partial grant. Like the P.S.O. grant, they are expected to remain constant in real terms for quite a few years.

On the question of more detailed objectives for the businesses and the railway passenger businesses and sectors in particular, there are many words but little detail. It is clear that the railway passenger P.S.O. cash limit will be modified to include the new £50 m rolling stock replacement grants. However, the requirements suggested in respect of the Railways businesses and sectors are not definite and will presumably have to be developed further.

On the Railways passenger side, the White Paper rules out any idea of imposing major cuts in the railway network. It does not suggest any positive objectives (other than the overall P.S.O. cash limit) in dealing with the individual sectors but does discuss the need to do this from 1978, in consultation with British Rail, although this is not yet achieved. It is explained that the targets will be set in terms of sectoral 'contributions' which will in due course be related to an avoidable costing basis.[6] It is not entirely clear what this means, but it may mean that the British Railways definition of 'contribution' will continue to be used until such time as British Rail can develop its costing procedures to establish the avoidable costs of each railway business and sector (within passenger), as discussed in chapter 6. This contribution is presently the difference between sector 'earnings', i.e. receipts allocated to sectors, and the direct costs of train working and terminals operation. The contribution refers to contribution to the joint costs of track and signalling, administration and interest. This appears to be a very satisfactory temporary measure and is considerably better than the previous unpublished notions of setting targets against so-called 'shares of the P.S.O.' by allocating the joint costs by arbitrary techniques associated with volume statistics. That process which has been discussed in more depth in chapter 6 does not lend itself to adequate monitoring and control. The suggested avoidable costs routine is in full agreement with the proposal made in the British Rail document *An Opportunity for Change* which was its response to the 1976 Green Paper.[7]

The White Paper gives some clues as to the likely levels of financial targets for the passenger sectors. In the Inter-city sector the suggestion is that these services should pay their way, and this means 'including a proper share of the cost of the infrastructure'.[8] There is no specific mention of administration or interest but presumably these are included. When figures, based on the allocation of joint costs, were quoted in the 1976 Green Paper, it was acknowledged that the Inter-city sector loss was approximately £15 m in 1976. It would seem rather likely that the avoidable joint costs of this sector are greater than the allocated share and the break-even target could prove to be quite a challenge, when it is eventually worked out. In the meantime, the degree of challenge represented by the provisional 'contribution' based targets will depend upon the outcome of the consultation procedures that are prescribed.

On the London and South East sector of the passenger business, the same target setting proposals will apply, and it is interesting to note that the 'allocated' share of the P.S.O. for 1976 given in the Green Paper in respect of this sector was approxiamtely £80 m per annum.[9]

It is impossible to pre-judge how this would change under 'avoidable' rules, and it is acknowledged that it will take a year or so to establish the costing procedures required to produce such an answer. The White Paper gives few clues on the likely targets for this sector but does announce that 'the government has decided not to impose on the Board a specific financial target for reducing the subsidy',[10] as was suggested in the 1976 Green Paper. Instead, there are remarks concerning the need to cut costs and phasing of price increases (presumably real price increases) to enable commuters to adjust to them. All this tends to suggest that the target will be to prevent a deterioration in the financial situation of this sector and perhaps make a small improvement.

There are fewer clues still in the White Paper about targets for the P.T.E. sector or the Other Provincial sector which the Green Paper described as accounting for over £128 m of the 1976 P.S.O. grant on an 'allocated' basis.[11] Instead, the emphasis in Cmnd 6836 is placed on local involvement in planning. It is proposed that the non-metropolitan county councils (sometimes described as shire counties) should be required to prepare five-year transport plans for their areas, in consultation with the transport operators.[12] These plans would include the transport services which require to be supported at county level. Further, their preparation will require cross-boundary consultation. This announcement adds to the situation which started under the provisions of section 203 of the *Local Government Act 1972* and the subsequent Department of the Environment directives.[13] Under those arrangements the shire counties were required to produce five-year 'transport policies and programmes' (T.P.P.s) on an annual basis to support their requirements for transport supplementary grants. The new procedures are required to work within that framework but ensure a more detailed examination of the public transport element and the creation of contractual arrangements between the shire counties and the transport operators.

However, within this framework, the White Paper makes an important proposal which is understood to be for discussion only, although little discussion has, in fact, taken place. It has been possible for many years for local authorities to provide grants to British Rail towards losses on selected services. T.P.P. arrangements invited this if a shire county council regarded such support as crucial to the development of a balanced transport policy within its area. Now it is tentatively proposed to put the onus on British Rail to declare which services would not be retained unless there was a strong local need for them. The White Paper explains that 'the Board would first apply a prima facie test, which would be publicly announced in terms of value for money'.[14] This will relate to the difference between identified receipts and avoidable costs, with the larger negative results presumably being the chosen services. Details of the services would then be considered by the Department of Transport to establish any overriding national (or political?) need, the absence of which requires that the service details be considered by the shire county council concerned. The county may then decide to support the service to the extent of the loss on the avoidable costs. This procedure might involve British Rail in having to deal with forty-seven counties in addition to the existing P.T.E. arrangements.

The distribution of the P.S.O. given in the 1976 Green Paper using the 'allocated' basis, when summed, falls considerably below the 1976 P.S.O. Ignoring differences caused by using approximate figures, the reason is the extent of the 'unavoidable' joint costs included in the P.S.O. because they were not 'avoidable' to the combined freight and parcels businesses. It will be remembered that the *Railways Act 1974* provided for those businesses to be charged with their avoidable costs (joint costs in practice, the share of direct costs being presumed to be equal to avoidable). This meant that the difference between the 'allocated' level and the 'avoidable' level would be included in the P.S.O. but not charged to any of the passenger sectors. This difference, known in British Rail circles as the basic facility cost or, for amusement, as 'the rump', is a considerable amount of money and is given in the Green Paper as 'over £100 m'.[15]

On the freight side, the White Paper confirms the need for the elimination of the subsidy in 1978. To assist in achieving this it is proposed that the government will maintain progress on ensuring that the taxation on lorries will be increased to cover the full costs of roads, including policing and accidents. Further they propose making an extra charge eventually to cover social and environmental costs, although these are difficult to assess.

Other proposals include the extension of the private siding grants to rail freight customers who can switch considerable traffic to rail[16] (see chapter 5 for original arrangements), the five-year rolling programme for construction of locomotives and wagons and 'eventual' introduction of the E.E.C. regulations on drivers' hours.[17] These proposals are made in association with the view that British Rail should 'concentrate on the jobs they do well'[18] and also make significant man-power reductions.[19] The 'jobs' in question are, of course, some of the activities such as the concentrated bulk flows and certain less than train load services where circumstances permit minimal resource requirements. Targets of future profitability are not suggested.

On the parcels side, the White Paper recognises, but does not seek to cure directly, a national over-capacity problem in this market sector. The proposal is to eliminate the grant in 1978 by a mixture of 'pricing, marketing and cost reduction',[20] as appropriate. Targets of future profitability are not suggested.

In regard to British Rail's other businesses, the White Paper makes a brief passing comment only. The proposal is merely to consider with the British Railways Board the ways in which obstacles towards a genuinely profitable future can be overcome and removed.[21] Presumably the break-even requirement will continue to apply.

The 1977 White Paper seems to provide a better basis for the determination of objectives than was the case hitherto. For most of his five years (1971–6) as Chairman of British Rail, Sir Richard Marsh was frequently and publicly asking government ministers to 'tell us what is expected of us'. The White Paper seems to go some way towards this, and with the help of considerable guidance from the sponsor department, every business board might now be expected to develop its own objectives. These would be determined through consultation and, in respect of the Railways business, would certainly relate to the sectors of the business. These proposed targets may be a bit uncertain and incomplete for a while, but they represent a major step in the right direction. They could provide the biggest and most useful impetus to corporate and financial planning in British Rail for many years.

There are unresolved deficiences in the White Paper. The first relates to the lack of clarity and precision in the proposed financial targets. This may be fair enough for the time being because the Department of Transport and British Rail will presumably attempt to become more precise through consultation. However, it seems quite possible that the end-product will still be deficient because it seems unlikely that 'profit' targets (involving avoidable costs perhaps) will be set for the freight and parcels businesses, or the passenger Inter-city sector. Further, there is no special mention of the new 'rump' which is created by putting each railway business and sector on the avoidable costs basis. It is clear within British Rail circles that it is considered that this new 'rump' may be quite large, perhaps approaching the order of the old rump. The White Paper does not consider the existence of this 'basic facility cost' or any targets concerning its development.

The second deficiency is the complete lack of attention paid to the non-railway businesses. As mentioned in chapter 4, these are large businesses in their own right. There should be no special reason for excluding them from the financial target setting process. They require clear objectives as much as the Railways business.

The third is the almost complete disregard for objectives of a non-financial nature. There is little mention of the levels of service which are required or the various aspects of the quality of that service. This is a surprising omission given that much of the Railways passenger business is concerned with services with significant social and environmental connections. The implicit attitude seems to be that the railway network is about the right size, British Rail is unlikely to want to make major service reductions and any problems concerning severely uneconomic services will be covered by the new arrangements with the shire counties.

However, there has been a further development in the area. The Price Commission report on the 1978 passenger fares increase pointed out that British Rail has an objective to maximise passenger miles within the constraint of the P.S.O. cash limit.[22] It would probably be more accurate to say that British Rail is considering such an objective, but it does not exist at the moment. Perhaps such an objective will emerge during the discussions on the sector financial targets for passenger miles being established. These would be more meaningful than an overall target. The question of developing a 'social fare' arises in this context, the idea being that each sector requires a government subsidy per passenger mile. However, it will take some time for British Rail and the Department of Transport to establish suitable objectives and procedures in this area. Care needs to be taken to ensure that the arrangements are compatible with the financial objectives and allow for contingencies, including pay settlements beyond budgeted levels.

The fourth and final deficiency may not in fact arise: this is that having determined the end, government will have to be associated with the means. Difficult decisions concerning real pricing, pay restraint, manpower reductions and, in some areas, service reductions may need to be taken if British Rail is to meet its targets. British Rail

management will rightly expect complete support in the announcement, union consultation and implementation of such decisions.

9.2 British Rail strategy

The corporate and financial planning theory outlined in chapter 2
stressed the need to proceed with the development of strategy after
determination of objectives, albeit with recycling as necessary. This
has been explained as amounting to determining the sense of purpose
before the sense of direction. In the light of the problems discussed so
far in this chapter, it would seem appropriate to comment that British
Rail, in association with government, have not cleared the first hurdle,
so they should not be expected to be attacking the second. However,
such an attitude is unrealistic, and it is clear that British Rail has been
developing its strategy in spite of the lack of clarity surrounding the
objectives. This may lead to many inadequacies but that is better than
no progress at all.

This section will discuss British Rail's strategy determination and
development. This will be undertaken within the context of the
Railways businesses as a whole and the passenger sectors. Three key
issues will then be specially considered; these are investment, passenger pricing and manpower productivity. The overall strategy for
British Railways is necessarily the co-ordinated sum of the strategy of
all its businesses. In turn the passenger sectors relate in total to the
Railways passenger business. Accordingly, it is advisable to start
our discussion at the bottom of the passenger pyramid with a brief
consideration of the strategy proposals and possibilities for each of
the sectors.

The strategy for the Inter-city sector of the Railways passenger
business is considered, within British Rail, to be one of the best
developed, in terms of the existence of a long-standing commitment
to a sense of direction. For the whole of the last decade, this has been
concerned with the development of fast and frequent services between
the cities and towns covered by the existing network with a high
quality of service measured in terms of punctuality, cleanliness, catering, interconnections and above all up-to-date equipment. The key
issue is investment, covering rolling stock, terminals (improvements
and some new facilities), maintenance facilities (mainly to cover the
new types of rolling stock) and infrastructure (where extensive elec-

trification is proposed). The planned capital investment contains two major proposals, i.e. the high speed trains and the advanced passenger trains.

By the end of the 1980s, British Rail hope to have introduced high speed trains or advanced passenger trains covering all primary services. Whilst not every Inter-city service will have the benefit of this advanced equipment, the proposals will benefit all of the services. This is because the secondary Inter-city services will utilise the newer rolling stock built during the last ten years which will no longer be required by the primary services. This process, which is known as 'cascading' within B.R. circles, will also benefit the freight business by providing a larger fleet of powerful locomotives more suited to the development of that business, thus facilitating the scrapping of a larger number of other types.

The Inter-city strategy is considered adventurous by British Rail and is motivated by a strong commercial attitude. The intention is to charge the market price for the improved services and this will inevitably mean considerable real pricing because the quality improvements are thought to have a significant effect on the market price. However, the expected major revenue change in constant prices will result from volume growth and not real pricing, and again this is associated with the product improvements.

We would not wish to give the impression that profits are predicted under this strategy which would change the overall financial outlook of British Rail. They are predicted to be quite healthy and might convert the current share of the loss covered by the P.S.O. (mentioned earlier as £15 m for 1976 using allocated costs) to a 'profit' level of about £20–50 m in 1978 prices within ten years (again using allocated costs for convenience), but that is all. Depending on the level of the avoidable costs which British Rail are now assessing (in place of the direct and allocated joint costs), it could well be that even that 'profit' will not exist. The reason is the high capital and maintenance costs of the rolling stock. The depreciation charges will be high and based on a fifteen-year life cycle for the H.S.T. and A.P.T. with an approximate capital cost of £1.6 m and £2.5 m for each respectively. To provide track and signalling suitable for the improved services, further increased revenue investment will be required and this will be a direct charge to working expenses for many years. The interest burden is not expected to rise to the extent that it otherwise would because of the new rolling stock grant proposals, but this is presently deficient and will remain so until the 'profits' reach the level predicted for the late 1980s.

It seems certain that the lack of clear objectives for the Inter-city sector has not mattered in the past. As to the future, the strategy seems to match the likely objectives in the shape of financial targets. This is not surprising because the B.R.B. has kept the Department of Transport fully informed of its ideas and has received no complaints in principle. Indeed, the tranches of H.S.T. investment so far submitted to the Department in terms of investment projects with D.C.F. appraisals have all received approval. The major problem will not arise until after 1980 when the government may not make the additional investment funds available. British Rail's plans provide for no overall increase in the annual level of investment spending up to 1980, in compliance with the investment ceiling requirements. However, beyond that year the Inter-city strategy depends heavily upon increased investment being available in total. British Rail do not propose to increase the Inter-city investment during the next ten years or so but the total capital investment may have to increase by as much as £30–60 m per annum beyond 1980 to meet the essential replacement requirements of the other passenger sectors and the freight business. If additional capital investment funds are not available, then it may well be that severe cutbacks may be required in the Inter-city investment because they are less practicable elsewhere. To a lesser degree the same situation applies to the revenue investment where about £20 m per annum is thought to be required in the way of additional investment beyond 1980. It will be noted at this stage that the investment grant prescribed in the 1977 White Paper (discussed earlier as being worth £50 m per annum) which has been described as too little to cover the existing rolling stock investment, becomes even more inadequate after 1980.

Because of an apparent lack of desire on the part of the government to make a long term commitment, the Department of Transport and British Rail have no agreement concerning the availability of borrowings associated with this increased investment. Thus, the strategy is uncertain in its detail, and the speed of introduction may need to be severely constrained. It is to be hoped that the negotiations which will take place concerning the objectives of this and other sectors will look beyond the next five years and encourage the Department to consider the longer-term strategic implications. Past experience suggests that reliance will be placed on shorter time-spans and that financial targets will probably be geared to the five years from 1980 to 1985. The problem will therefore remain unresolved for some considerable time.

In the London and South East sector strategic matters have been considered, but there are no firm proposals apart from some essential replacement of rolling stock in the mid and late 1980s; nor will there be until the financial targets are thrashed out. During the two years prior to the publication of the 1977 White Paper it was apparent that the Department of Transport wished to set objectives for this sector which would significantly reduce its share of the P.S.O. grant. They commissioned a B.R.B. study of the sector to establish the strategy required to make this happen by selective action in each of its three nominated sub-sectors. This study showed that the 'inner' services (about fifteen miles radius around London) would be required to make small reductions in their share of the P.S.O., the 'outer' services (all other services to London) would be required to eliminate their share within three to five years and the 'peripheral' services (services within the area but not serving London) would be required to maintain their share at constant levels.

The B.R.B. study showed that the most important element needed to meet this requirement was substantial real pricing, i.e. considerably beyond the level of inflation. Aspects of the report were contained in the B.R. response *An Opportunity for Change* to the 1976 Green Paper. The suggestion was that real pricing of 7½% for five years (i.e. price increases of 7½% over and above the Retail Prices Index for each of those years) would be required and that this would mean considerable customer resistance estimated to produce a 15% decline in passenger journeys by the fifth year.[23] The government found it impossible to accept the implications of these proposals, and this has resulted in the acceptance in the White Paper of the need to perpetuate the existing level of subsidies.

Thus for the London and South East sector there are no formal objectives in existence and there is no real strategy at present. The negotiations between the Department and B.R.B. concerning the financial targets should be extremely interesting. They may lead to a desire for containment of the grant. This will require a small level of real pricing annually to pay for any real cost increases (notably real staff cost escalation) which will arise plus increases in depreciation (arising from the replacement investment) and major increases in maintenance resulting from using older rolling stock. Cost reductions will be a prime requirement but they are not easily obtained in this sector. This is a result of the lack of flexibility in restructuring the services because of the heavy demand for services at some times during the day; that is, a 'peaked demand' problem.

It is unlikely that the strategy will include investment beyond projects of an essential replacement nature. This is partly because of the investment ceilings up to 1983. After this, there may be an additional problem arising out of the lack of profitable investment. It is not considered that the market will respond to major investment in this sector, but it will suffer what many users regard as the present inadequate quality of service at a high price because those presently travelling represent a partially captive market. This unhappy situation may have to continue for many years and is unlikely to be changed by the 1977 White Paper proposals.

The P.T.E. sector is a little more satisfactory but here again it cannot be said that a complete strategy exists. Each of the P.T.E.s has developed its new investment proposals as a result of developing specific proposals to deal with local problems. Also, British Rail has plans for some essential rolling stock replacement in the mid and late 1980s. However, the P.T.E.s are inclined to take a short-term view generally, being concerned more about next year's P.T.E. grant than five or ten year objectives and strategy. This applies particularly to pricing but also to investment where an overall strategic assessment does not exist. The 1977 White Paper does not help much directly in this area. However, the P.T.E.s seem to be aware of potential problems and have commenced discussions with British Rail about their longer-term aims and proposals, at least covering a three-year period.

The Other Provincial sector has been a strategic non-event. There are no proposals and little planned investment, again other than for essential rolling stock replacement. Here again everything depends on the development of the financial targets. However, in this area the emphasis is likely to be placed on the need for cost reductions, with little real pricing capability existing. Further there may possibly be cautious implementation of the proposals to involve the shire counties in making direct grants on an avoidable costs basis. It is unlikely that British Rail will wish to jump headlong into this process since this would produce a large list of service closure proposals for the forty-seven shire counties to consider supporting as an alternative to closure. Thus, it seems likely that the development of strategy in this sector will be a very slow process and may take as long as two to three years, even assuming that the financial targets will be settled in that time.

When added together, it can be seen that there is much uncertainty concerning the development of the financial element of the strategy for the passenger business. A great deal of this uncertainty will disappear when the financial targets are agreed but much work still requires to be done. It may well be that what will emerge is a strategy of continued modernisation within the Inter-city sector and merely a holding operation elsewhere with some real price increases (L. & S.E. sector) and cost reductions where possible. However, much of the detail at least will depend on the results of the continuing passenger sectoral strategic study.

As far as the Railways freight business is concerned, it is apparent that this is an area which has had even more strategic attention paid to it than the passenger Inter-city sector. During the last ten years there has been a major and deliberate shift of emphasis towards a concentration on its train load sector with significant run-down in the less than train load sector. This has produced immense benefits in terms of utilisation of resources which has been further improved by computer assisted control of rolling stock disposition.

In the last three years, British Rail has conducted a fresh examination of the freight strategy. Basically, two extremes of alternative courses of action are possible. The first accepts that the basic freight network and resources are roughly right and attempts to market within that system, partly by using marginal costs as a price criterion of acceptability. The second proposes a considerable reduction in the 'less than train load' sector to establish a limited system serving major conurbations without intermediate marshalling and using higher speed air-braked wagons, with very limited local feeder services. A steady increase in train load traffic is likely in either case. The latter extreme would be an attempt at specialisation and involve full acceptance of the principle that the Railways freight business should only carry traffic to which it is best suited, i.e. long distance, heavy traffic with intensive asset utilisation. Firm decisions have not been made in this area, but it is apparent from the 1977 White Paper that the government seem to be leaning towards the second extreme requiring British Rail to 'concentrate on the jobs it does well'. A less rigorous approach is likely to emerge but one with a sufficient degree of change to produce a freight business which can make a very adequate return on capital employed. The first extreme will probably not work because of the immense variety of flows which make resource utilisation optimisation difficult to obtain and adequate utilisation (from a financial point of view) impossible.

Such a freight strategy would involve shedding some traffic to road, even if over the next few years British Rail see good prospects of expanding the train load sector. This may not be acceptable from a social point of view or from the point of view of the nation as a whole. The final freight strategy will be designed to meet financial targets. If these are acceptable, it seems likely that British Rail will have a clear freight strategy within the near future and that this may have a considerable bearing on the determinaiton of the financial targets for that business. These may involve a continuation of the current 'break-even' requirement or an ambitious profit target. The latter will involve resource reductions of a high order, including manpower savings.

It is not difficult to predict what sort of strategy might be developed for the parcels business in the next few years. As mentioned earlier, the White Paper dismisses any fundamental changes such as closing down the unprofitable 'collected and delivered' sector by transferring the traffic to the Post Office and National Freight Corporation. Thus, the present concentration of pricing and marketing policies with cost reductions is likely to continue as the only practical alternative. They may be adequate for a few years but they are unlikely to provide profits which could be regarded as making any significant return on the capital employed.

The parcels share of the 1978 freight and parcels loss (i.e. temporary grant) is broadly assessed at £2 m, using the avoidable approach to joint costs which, as mentioned earlier, has been used for the combined freight and parcels business since 1975. It is thought, within British Rail, that this loss is broadly made up of a large loss for the 'collected and delivered' sector and a slightly smaller profit for the so-called 'station to station' sector. It is not practical for British Rail to assess these figures properly because this would involve an immense amount of arbitrary allocation which would only result in spurious accuracy. The 'station to station' profit is somewhat artificial because much of the traffic in that sector is given a free ride on passenger trains and some of its costs are therefore contained within the P.S.O. The costs of the 'collected and delivered' sector are more realistic and the estimated loss is thought to be quite disproportionate to a turnover of about £60 m.

In the light of these remarks, it seems inadequate for the government to require the elimination of the total loss from 1978 as their only proposal. British Rail confidently predict that this will be achieved for a few years by using the prescribed methods of pricing, marketing and cost reductions. However, it is doubtful whether they can hold the situation for many years, and the continued erosion of traffic to 'owners haul' and fierce road and Post Office price competition are likely to eliminate the break-even capability in a few years and push the parcels business back into making small losses by the mid 1980s. Erosion of some of the 'collected and delivered' traffic could be useful in that it will facilitate cost reductions in some locations by restructuring of services and facilities, but significant reductions cannot be matched by equivalent cost reductions and will create losses. It seems likely that the Department of Transport will set a break-even target for the next three to five years and this is likely to be achieved.

Summarising the situation for the railways business, it is clear that a great deal of strategic activity is going to take place during the next couple of years. It is interesting to reflect on the fact that this is almost entirely in connection with what we have described as the financial element of strategy. The primary preoccupation will be the development of 'means' to satisfy financial 'ends'. There are likely to be few or no non-financial objectives for some time and the strategy will be financially orientated even in areas of service quality because they are not the truly desired 'ends', only the 'means' of arriving at financial ends. Thus, to repeat a point made much earlier, in British Rail financial planning is the only real aspect of corporate planning. All of the other aspects such as production planning and manpower planning become subservient because there are no non-financial objectives.

In the light of these general comments, we can now look at the three special railway strategic issues mentioned earlier in a little more depth. The first issue is railway investment which is currently running at about £300 m per annum (average 1978 prices), covering both revenue and capital investment. This figure is, of course, the Railways share of the ceiling figure which it is understood must be maintained for a few years. Beyond the mid 1980s British Rail planners are hoping that a considerable but gradual increase is possible to a level of about £350 m by the later years of the decade. As mentioned earlier, this increased investment is meant to sustain the current level of passenger Inter-city investment, whilst at the same time providing for essential replacements elsewhere.

The problem is that the level of replacement becoming essential is likely to increase alarmingly after the late 1980s in all areas, particularly rolling stock and infrastructure. This will result from the fact that the level of investment in the last fifteen years has been hopelessly less than a level which might be described as self-sustaining. It is broadly estimated that the self-sustaining level of investment is between £350 m and £400 m, even allowing for the resource reductions suggested earlier. It is estimated that the current depreciation charge is only 20% of that which would be required on a replacement cost basis. This is partly a result of inflation but also a consequence of a 'make do and mend' attitude to satisfy government constraints and the level of declared profits or losses.

Beyond the mid 1980s investment would need to increase or else the 'rotting railway' syndrome might be expected to become a reality. It is probably quite fair to say that the 'make do and mend' principle has been a good discipline because it has helped to ensure that a strong case is made for all investment within the limited funds. This discipline is likely to continue because there can be no possibility of any investment floodgates being opened. Instead, it is recommended that the investment level be allowed to rise to about £350 m (in 1978 prices) by about 1985. Beyond 1985 it seems likely that only small increases will be required, with the 'make do and mend' philosophy being continued, particularly through refurbishment of rolling stock where this is a practical alternative to replacement.

There is no evidence to support the suggestion made by the railway unions that the current investment ceiling will itself cause any immediate significant problems such as service reductions. Only if the situation continues for many years will this possibility arise but even then it is more likely that the 'make do and mend' process will be further stretched and some of the cuts will be made in the Inter-city high speed development programme. Thus, it is predicted that the Railways would not show serious signs of 'rotting' for about ten years. But, by then, the investment needed to recover the situation during the succeeding ten years would be considerably more than the required level of £350–400 m per annum if the high speed programme is to survive and all essential replacement is to take place.

None of this will be of comfort to the London and South East commuter or the users of some of the other services using old assets ideally in need of replacement. Most of the locomotives are nearing the end of their book lives, as are the coaches and multiple units. There is no doubt that they can be maintained well beyond their book lives but not with the same degree of maintenance cost or quality of service. However, we must repeat that the only present requirement placed on British Rail by the government is an uncertain level of financial performance. The quality of that performance or its level in terms of passenger miles or journeys is not a prime criterion for assessment of achievement of objectives; in reality they are only influences on the financial objectives. This situation may continue for some time, given that the 1977 White Paper does not recognise the need for non-financial objectives.

The development of the required rate of return on capital investment in chapter 8 is unlikely to have a major effect. The White Paper on the nationalised industries makes it clear that the 5% return on the overall investment should not apply to a nationalised industry providing a social service. Given the P.S.O. grant arrangements, the British Rail passenger business must fall within that context (perhaps excluding the Inter-city sector) and will presumably have a nil rate of return. On the combined freight and parcels side, investment is not the key to success, and it is thought that the strategy emerging from the freight studies combined with the results of the parcels study when completed may well produce profit forecasts which provide a 5% return on the new investment.

The concentration on financial objectives as a sole government criterion for measurement of success has a major bearing on the next key issue–passenger pricing. It must be emphasised at the outset that the purpose of all pricing action taken by railways management is to go a long way towards maximisation of revenue. The philosophy of market pricing through selective price increases is presently not taken to its limits, being modified by such things as public opinion, government opinion and the immediate cash limit situation.

An absurd example of such a pricing policy–made only for the purpose of illustration–would be if British Rail were to concentrate on just 100 000 customers who might be willing to pay £10 000 each for their annual journeys. All of the other millions of customers would represent the resistance to price increases and cease to travel by rail. In these circumstances, British Rail would be able to reduce the service levels to the needs of their 100 000 customers, make a handsome profit and have no cash limit problems. In the absence of non-financial objectives they could demonstrate that they had fulfilled their remit.

That example may be absurd but it is indicative of the rationale which presently exists. The government may consider that the size of the Railways passenger network is about right but they have no apparent view presently on the number of journeys or passenger miles which should occur. The only criterion, and a hazy one at that, in terms of its sectoral distribution, is the level of P.S.O. grant which can be allowed to arise. In these circumstances it is absolutely essential for British Rail to be quite bold in determining price increases and constantly strive to keep reasonably near to the market price.

The effect of this has been described in chapter 4 in the shape of reductions in passenger journeys or miles in some years caused by large price increases. It is very difficult to measure the resistance accurately because it is a constantly changing situation and affected by a number of variables other than price, including the general level of inflation. However, we consider that the current situation is that it is necessary to increase prices by about 1 or 2% above R.P.I. in order to achieve a net annual price increase equal to the general rate of inflation. This means that a 1 or 2% loss of patronage would not decrease the total revenue coming into the British Rail purse. As mentioned earlier, this resistance will arise, in the main, in the Inter-city and Other Provincial sectors.

Such pricing action does not achieve the market price but goes a long way towards it. In the London and South East sector, the market price is considerably above today's price levels but the political impli-cations of going that far are considerable. The idea has been rejected in the 1977 White Paper and its consequences will be seen in the target setting process. In the other sectors current prices are considered to be much closer to the market price.

The National Union of Railwaymen has tried in the past to suggest that further price increases of the same order as the inflation rate were not required. They have suggested a price freeze and even price reductions, suggesting that increased patronage would result, pro-ducing the required level of receipts. This is a naive solution which does not recognise the vital nature of matching inflation, at least, with price increases. From analyses already carried out, it is reasonably clear that volume could not increase by anything like the same amount in those circumstances. The only chance of achieving small price increases lies in there being a low general rate of inflation coupled with low Railways costs inflation.

These remarks may seem to suggest that we are predicting a small reduction in passenger volume during the next few years until inflation is brought down to a small annual percentage. In fact this is not the case because the price resistance volume reductions are forecast to be more than offset by volume increases caused by service improvements. These service improvements are, of course, concentrated mainly in the Inter-city sector and relate mainly to the high speed development. Thus, the volume reduction experienced in 1976 will not be repeated in total despite continued price resistance. Some people will not travel by rail because the price becomes too high whilst their neighbours will make new journeys because the product has improved.

But of course, the level of the P.S.O. grant has as much to do with costs as it has with receipts, as does the level of freight and parcels profit or loss. This leads us to deal with the third key issue—manpower productivity. The public at large considers that the Railways are over-manned and could reduce their manpower by anything up to one-quarter. Such a reduction would have a major bearing on the financial results. It would not eliminate the P.S.O. but would convert the combined freight and parcels businesses from their current loss into profit. The British Railways Board considered that it was quite feasible to reduce the Railways' manpower by 40 000 during the five years from 1976 to 1980 inclusive. This target time has since been modified to about 1983. The 1980 target is quoted in the B.R. publication *An Opportunity for Change*[24] and, whilst it is some 12 000 short of the one-quarter figure (including B.R.E.L.), it still represents a major task which will be fought every inch of the way by the railway unions. It would be naive to assume that if the Railways could be run by 40 000 fewer staff, then this reduction should be immediately achieved. The consultation processes are long and arduous and involve producing changes in services and rationalisation of yards, depots and terminals to increase utilisation realistically. In addition to being a slow process for these reasons, there is one overriding factor and that is whatever is done will be done without compulsory dismissal. This ties the manpower reductions to the levels of natural wastage, and it was this issue which led to the original timing of the proposed 40 000 reduction. It was considered by British Rail that natural wastage together with their productivity proposals and their union consultation requirements could produce a reduction of 8000 per annum at the most.

Pryke and Dodgson identified what they considered to be scope for a massive reduction in staff by 1981 resulting from a host of items,[25] which British Rail had, by and large, already considered. These included such issues as train miles, loads and speeds changes, driving time improvements, need for secondmen and freight guards, ticket inspection on trains, automatic ticket inspection, reduced station staff resulting from power doors in trains and extension of automatic signalling. Their approach was far too cavalier, although a number of the items are still being examined with a view to staged introduction. The 40 000 target represents the maximum that British Rail considers it can achieve by 1983. We consider that a further 10 000 can be achieved by the end of the 1980s dependent upon high investment and the detailed results of the sectoral strategic studies. But this would need to be varied if there were to be a shorter working week. A total of 50 000 would be much less than the Pryke and Dodgson figure, and even this would only be achieved much later than they suggested.

A reduction of 50 000 by 1981 or even 1983 from the level at the beginning of 1976 is not possible. Indeed, results since 1976 confirm that British Rail will not achieve the 40 000 reduction until well into the 1980s. In 1976 the Railways business manpower reduction was 7236 with a further 4456 in 1977. There was practically no reduction in 1978. Much will depend on the 1980 pay negotiations and its productivity 'strings'. The B.R.B. is hoping that a productivity deal will mean that the consultative processes will be speeded up and in some cases recommenced and that the annual manpower reduction will reach the 8000 level.

The cost reduction which the manpower savings would produce will not necessarily mean that customer pricing action will not need to be as severe as discussed earlier in this section. Instead, it will offset the increases in depreciation, interest, rolling stock maintenance and revenue investment which are bound to arise. Also, it will have to pay for any increases in real staff costs, bearing in mind that the 'going-rate' for pay awards will not, in the long run, be set by British Rail, but by the general level of pay settlements. However, the extent to which price increases can be mitigated will depend mainly on the cash limits and financial targets which will emerge in coming months.

TEN

Latest Developments

This concluding chapter is concerned with bringing elements of the book up to date. As will have been observed, the earlier chapters reflected the situation up to, or as at, the summer of 1979. This chapter takes matters up to spring 1980.

It is not considered necessary to deal further with the theoretical content but, instead, with the British Rail exemplary material, where there is much to add. To do this, we have used three headings which cover the financial situation, the development of objectives and strategy and a summarised comparison with the normative corporate planning model. The third heading is not so much an update as a set of concluding observations.

10.1 British Rail–financial situation

The year 1979 was not a good one for British Rail, particularly in respect of the Railways business. The results, in a form suitable for updating tables 5.5 and 5.6, are given on the next page.

At first sight, the 1979 Railways business result does not look much different to that for 1978, although it will be appreciated that, as in earlier years, the Railways business incurs the bulk of the overall interest burden. The big problem area was the disproportionate increase in the P.S.O. grant. This was forecast to arise in chapter 5 (section 5.2) and resulted largely from the imbalance of passenger fares increases and cost increases. Passenger fares were increased by 9% in January 1979 when it was anticipated that the April 1979 pay settlement would be much lower than the final deal of approximately 13%, overall, turned out to be. Additionally, fuel oil increases were

Table 5.5   B.R.B. consolidated profit-and-loss account–1979

	£m
Surplus/(Deficit) of each activity	
Railways	34.2
Ships	9.6
Harbours	4.0
Hotels	0.3
Non-operational property	7.3
Hovercraft	(0.8)
B.R.E.L.	1.0
Freightliner	2.0
	57.6
Ancillary income	8.2
Corporate expenses	3.5
Surplus/(Deficit) before interest	62.3
Interest and exchange losses/(gains)	60.8
Taxation	0.1
Surplus/(Deficit) after interest	1.4
Extraordinary item	1.8
Adjusted surplus/(Deficit) after interest	(0.4)

Table 5.6   Railway business profit-and-loss account–1979

	£m
Receipts	
Passenger – Fares	799.7
– Grants (P.S.O. incl. P.T.E.)	522.5
Freight	432.1
Parcels	130.8
Miscellaneous	20.5
	1905.6
Working expenses	1888.9
	16.7
Ancillary income	17.5
Surplus/(Deficit) before interest	34.2

much higher than anticipated.

Overall, for the Railways business, receipts pricing action produced £136 m (passenger £68 m, freight £54 m and parcels £14 m). Pay and other cost increases amounted to £214 m. The difference has largely ended up as an increase in the level of the P.S.O. grant. The volume of receipts increased by £23 m, with a passenger improvement of £30 m having been offset by a reduction £4 m and £3 m in freight and parcels, respectively. This result would have been better by about £14 m (passenger £10 m, freight £4 m) were it not for the A.S.L.E.F. train drivers' dispute in January 1979. The volume of working expenses increased by £37 m, including a large increase (£29 m) in engineering workload.

This result has had a major impact on the P.S.O. cash limit situation. The 'headroom' dropped to only £14 m in 1979 (on the assumption that the P.S.O. grant was £530 m, after allowing for previous year adjustments), thus not auguring well for 1980. Further, the non-passenger 'break-even' cash limit was not achieved in 1979 and a loss of £2 m was recorded causing a borrowing requirement. Although the P.S.O. grant was within the cash limit level, it was £38 m above the budget which the Board regard as the 'contract' level. Thus, for the first time, the contract has been exceeded and by a very wide margin. However, much of the difference has been caused by price/cost variations rather than volume factors.

The Board's overall 1979/80 fiscal year 'financing' cash limit of £715 m mentioned in section 5.2 was achieved but not without considerable emergency action and anxiety. During the six months ended March 1980, reductions were made in investment and maintenance spending, minor pay increases were postponed, recruitment was temporarily halted (for about two months) and efforts made to improve working capital balances and to speed up the programmed disposal of property and other assets, where possible.

The prospects for the year 1980 and the fiscal year 1980/81 are rather bleak. The 1980 P.S.O. grant may need to be higher than its cash limit but the Government are not likely to allow the grant to exceed the laid down level and further emergency action will be required. Much will depend upon the level of fuel prices and the effect of productivity improvements relating to the latest (April 1980) pay deal which amounted to approximately 20%, with a productivity element. The January 1980 passenger fares increase was approximately 18% and the Board anticipated, and have so far achieved, a net yield of about 16% (i.e. 2% resistance). It is likely that this net yield will level out at about 17% which may prove to be inadequate to fund the pay increase, unless there are early productivity improvements. Consequently, further emergency action may be necessary in the second half of 1980 including, possibly, an autumn fares increase. The situation will be exacerbated by the further cuts in the P.S.O. cash limit amounting to £28 m (in 1980 prices) proposed in Cmnd 6836[1] (£19 m) and Cmnd 7841[2] (£9 m). There will also be continued effects, into 1981 of £21 m (in anticipated 1981 prices).

The 'easy' option of further postponement of investment is not favoured by B.R. management since it aggravates the long term asset replacement problem and much of the track renewal requirement cannot continue being postponed without causing deterioration in the services and/or changes in the levels of service provision. However, even investment reductions are likely.

On the non-passenger side, the 1980 price increases are likely to be much closer to the cost increases, given the greater flexibility of the freight and parcels market situations (i.e. separate price negotiations with large customers or index-linked price increases). A small profit would probably have been earned in 1980 were it not for the British Steel Corporation strike. That strike has reduced Railways receipts by about £28 m and will almost certainly produce a loss, which will again need to be covered by borrowings. The situation will be seriously aggravated by the recent downward trends in the freight and parcels markets caused by the general state of the national economy. Overall, a large non-passenger loss (even as much as £50 m) seems quite likely and the B.R.B. may again be seeking special financial assistance from government, at least to compensate for the BSC strike element.

The 1980/81 'financing' cash limit may prove to be as big a problem as the 1980 P.S.O. cash limit. The limit is set at £750 m. This is actually £160 m higher than the 1979/80 limit of £715 m since the pensions grant of £125 m (including interest) in 1979/80 has now been excluded from the calculations. This is because the Government now wishes to fund the deficiency at the time the money is required for pension payments rather than as required under the *Railway Act 1974*. This considerable postponement of funding is currently being dealt with in Parliament as one of the elements of the Transport Bill 1979. Again, much will depend on the level of passenger price increases, but whatever action is taken to achieve the 1980 P.S.O. cash limit, it will naturally benefit the 1980/81 financing situation.

One might reasonably wonder why British Rail has not overcome its recent financial problems by adequate fares increases. With the benefit of hindsight, we are bound to observe that once a 13% (approximately, overall) pay deal was negotiated in April 1979 a second fares increase in the second half of 1979 would have been an appropriate solution, particularly in the light of growing general inflation. The January 1980 fares increase was even lower than the likely average inflation level for 1980. This may mean that the net yield could in fact eventually reach the gross increase level of 18%, but even this will probably prove to be inadequate.

However, it is generally acknowledged in British Rail circles that the Board and its managers are reluctant to impose two passenger fares increases in any calendar year, mainly because of market reasons and of the attendant adverse publicity. The increases in 1975 and 1976 produced considerable criticism. Further, the incoming Conservative Government in the second half of 1979, was keen to keep nationalised industry prices down and has urged the Board not to have more than one increase per year and to keep the increases as low as possible. They also, incidentally, changed their departmental structure slightly and the position of Minister of Transport was re-created in place of Secretary of State for the Department of Transport.

Thus, the pressures from Government, explicit and implicit, have been proved contradictory and the absence of a second passenger fares incease in 1979 may prove to have been a considerable misjudgement. The chances of there not being a second passenger fares increase in the autumn of 1980 are rather slim.

In all this, one might also reasonably ask what happened to productivity in 1979. The April 1979 pay deal had productivity 'strings' in lieu of the 13% payment. These were meant to 'open up some of the doors' that had slowed down or even prevented the consultation machinery from producing significant manpower reductions since 1977. These 'strings' have been proven inoperable and the consultation process has not returned to the required degree of cooperation. Consequently, the Board have negotiated a much more definitive agreement as part of the 1980 pay deal. It remains to be seen how the productivity elements will turn out. Certainly, they are ambitious and cover actions which will stretch over the next two or three years. It is unlikely, however, that much financial benefit will accrue to the Railways business in what remains of 1980.

In summary, we have to observe that there has been a considerable deterioration in the finances of British Rail since the beginning of 1979, Coupled with tighter Government cash limits, this deterioration will, for some time, occupy the attention of the Board and its managers far more than the longer term financial planning considerations. Tommorrow's problems always give way to today's emergencies.

10.2. British Rail—development of objectives and strategy

It was stated at the beginning of section 6.2 of chapter 6 that, within British Rail, the financial planning activities represent the entire area of practice of the process of corporate planning, given that no attempt has been made to develop non-financial objectives. That position has not changed up to April 1980, although some progress has been made at setting financial objectives over and above those already mentioned, i.e. mainly the various cash limits and the break-even requirement of the non-passenger sector and the non-railway businesses. In fact, agreement has recently been reached with the Department of Transport on three fronts[3]:

(1) That the Inter-city Passenger sector should improve its 'contribution' to indirect expenses from £105 m to £133 m, in 1979 prices, by 1982.
(2) That the freight sector of the Railways non-passenger business should achieve a profit by 1982 after allowing for two-thirds of the depreciation which would be charged to that sector under current cost accounting (C.C.A.) rules.
(3) That Sealink U.K. Ltd should achieve by 1982 a 5% return on net assets at current cost.

This is a major step forward and one which will be repeated in respect of the other businesses/sectors in due course. Progress has been slow but is being made. The targets are very tough and call for finalisation and implementation of the the passenger 'sectoral' strategic study and the freight strategic study.

The objectives are timely in that the passenger strategic study is more or less finalised and strategic direction will shortly be provided. The details are currently being discussed with government. The freight sector strategic development is further advanced and attention is concentrated on the development of an action plan, although this is proving to be a lengthy process. Additionally, the parcels strategic study is almost completed.

At the same time, Sealink U.K. Ltd, British Transport Hotels Ltd,

Freightliners Ltd and B.R. Hovercraft Ltd, are all completing their strategic reviews and will shortly produce their decisions on future development.

Over and above the strategic development mentioned above, the Board has concluded its Channel Tunnel feasibility study in conjunction with S.N.C.F. and has produced a proposal for a single-bore tunnel at a cost of £650 m (in 1/1/78 prices) which is forecast to produce a good rate of return. This has met with considerable acclaim and enthusiasm, although the government are unwilling to provide the investment funds. The hope is that the E.E.C. or even private capital will eventually be provided.

The major electrification study is also nearing completion but, when available, may not be capable of speedy implementation because of a lack of government funds. As was clear in section 10.1, a measure of belt-tightening is seemingly required in the near future which will prevent an early start on heavy investment in electrification, however well justified.

However, notwithstanding these developments, there is also the prospect of 'privatisation' now being mooted by the Minister of Transport, whereby it is being suggested that Sealink U.K. Ltd, B.R. Property Board, British Transport Hotels Ltd and B.R. Hovercraft Ltd be sold off (wholly or partly) to the private sector. A holding company for these four business is being tentatively proposed, but detailed arrangements have not yet been made.

10.3 British Rail and the normative corporate planning model

In the light of this study of British Rail, three main conclusions may be drawn, which the latter part of the text deals with in some detail. The first is that the actuality of corporate planning in British Rail is different in degree to that of the normative model outlined in chapter 2. In particular, there are omissions at the objectives, strategy and action plans stage. With respect to objectives, there has been considerable recent progress, as outlined in section 10.2 but, overall, progress has been disappointing in the development of unambiguous long term objectives and a related strategy with full agreement between British Rail and government. Further, corporate planning in British Rail is dominated by financial planning with little regard being paid to the non-financial aspects, particularly the development of non-financial objectives.

The second conclusion is that, overall, progress has been slow in respect of the development of corporate planning in British Rail even to its current state. It has taken British Rail a decade to develop its corporate planning processes and mechanism to the present position which remains a considerable way from the normative model although it compares favourably with other large industries. This is not too surprising when one considers the size of the task and the immense difficulties, particularly in connection with the need to have agreement with government at all the vital stages.

However, at least there has been progress which has produced significant advantages. One advantage has been the consequential creation of an extra monitoring mechanism. A more important advantage, however, has been the development of a more meaningful dialogue between the Board and government made possible by the availability of more information. Indeed, it has facilitated the discussion on alternative courses of action which would not otherwise have been possible.

The third conclusion is that the model itself is not complete as it needs to be. Even if British Rail had had at their disposal the normative model from the outset, progress would still have been slower than might have been anticipated. This is because the model does not give sufficient guidance to organisations on how to develop their 'needs' in relation to their specific characteristics. In case of British Rail, the most important characteristic is that it is nationalised which, in turn implies that it has had to learn to handle a sometimes difficult and delicate relationship with government. This has meant that B.R. has, by and large, planned in relation to 'constraints' rather than 'needs'. It is to be hoped that government will use more wisely the output of the corporate planning processes of the nationalised industries and there are signs that this may be taking place. In particular, the advent of longer term planning horizons, rather than short term reactions should be encouraged.

Also, in the light of experience it is clear that, with an organisation like British Rail, with many diverse businesses, the emphasis in the normative model could be changed. Instead, of the development of an overall corporate objective and strategy to which the various parts have to correspond, it is clear that there can be major benefits to be gained by allowing the separate parts to assess their own objectives and strategies which, when aggregated, would form the overall corporate position.

References

Chapter 1
1. Pryke, Richard and Dodgson, John (1975) *The Rail Problem*. Martin Robertson.
2. *Transport Policy: A Consultation Document* **1** and **2** (1976). H.M.S.O.
3. British Railways Board (1976) *Transport Policy: An Opportunity for Change. Comments by British Railways Board on the Government Consultation Document.*
4. Cmnd 6836 (1977) *Transport Policy*. H.M.S.O.
5. National Economic Development Office (1976) *A Study of the U.K. Nationalised Industries. Their Role in the Economy and Control in the Future*. H.M.S.O.
6. Cmnd 7131 (1978) *The Nationalised Industries*. H.M.S.O.
7. *A Study of the U.K. Nationalised Industries. Their Role in the Economy and Control in the Future.* 24.
8. Grinyer, Peter H. and Wooller, Jeff (1975) *Corporate Models Today: A New Tool for Financial Management*. The Institute of Chartered Accountants in England and Wales. 176.
9. *ibid*. 200.
10. *Transport Policy: A Consultation Document* **1**, 49.
11. *The Rail Problem*. 252.
12. *ibid*.

Chapter 2
1. See, for example, Harris, D.J. (1978) 'Corporate Planning and Operational Research'. *Journal of Operational Research* **29**, 9–17.

2. Eden, Colin and Harris, John (1975) *Management Decisions and Decision Analysis*. Macmillan.
3. See, for example, Ansoff, H. Igor (1971) *Corporate Strategy*. Pelican Library of Business and Management. and Argenti, John (1968) *Corporate Planning, A Practical Guide*. George Allen and Unwin.
4. Ansoff, H. I. (1971) 'Strategy as a Tool for Coping with Change'. *Journal of Business Policy* **1** (4), 3.
5. *Corporate Strategy*. 32–35.
6. For a full explanation of 'organisational slack' see Cyert, Richard M. and March, James G. (1963) *A Behavioural Theory of the Firm*. Prentice Hall. 36–38.
7. *Corporate Models Today: A New Tool for Financial Management.*

Chapter 3

1. See, for example, Stonier, A. W. and Hague, D. C. (1953) *A Textbook of Economic Theory*. Longmans.
2. Wood, Douglas and Fildes, Robert (1976) *Forecasting for Business, Methods and Application*. Longman Business Series.
3. Chambers, J. C., Mullick, S. K. and Smith, D. D. (July–August 1971) 'How to Choose the Right Forecasting Technique'. *Harvard Business Review*.
4. Anthony, Robert N. and Herslinger, Regina (1975) *Management Control in Non-Profit Organisations*. Richard D. Irwin Inc. 227–228.
5. Hague, D. C. (1971) *Managerial Economics: Analysis for Business Decisions*. Longman Business Series. 218–220.
6. Lerner, E. M. and Rappaport, A. (September–October 1968) 'Limit D.C.F. in Capital Budgeting'. *Harvard Business Review*. 133–139.
7. Carsberg, Bryan (1974) *Analysis for Investment Decisions*. Accountancy Age Books. Chapter 8.

Chapter 4

1. British Rail/McKinsey and Co. Joint Report (1971) *Restructuring the Railway Field Organisation*. Internal report to British Rail.

Chapter 6

1. *Corporate Models Today: A New Tool for Financial Management.*

2. Cooper Brothers report (1967) *Corporate Planning in British Railways.* Internal report to British Rail.
3. *ibid.*, 3, para 13.
4. *Transport Policy: A Consultation Document* **1.**
5. Cmnd 6836.
6. *Transport Act 1962.* H.M.S.O.
7. *Transport Act 1968.* H.M.S.O.
8. *Railways Act 1974.* H.M.S.O. 2.
9. *Transport Policy: An Opportunity for Change.* 35.
10. British Railways Board (1978) *Measuring Cost and Profitability in British Rail.*
11. Cmnd 3656 (1968) *Proposed Increases by British Railways Board in Country-wide Fares and Charges.* N.B.P.I. Report 72.

Chapter 7
1. Cmnd 3439 (1967) *Railway Policy.*
2. *Transport Act 1968.*
3. House of Commons Report 371 (1968) *First Report from the Select Committee on Nationalised Industries, Session 1967/68, Ministerial Control of the Nationalised Industries.*
4. *ibid.*, chapter XVIII.
5. *A Study of the U.K. Nationalised Industries. Their Role in the Economy and Control in the Future.* 24.
6. House of Commons Report 305 (1977) *First Report from the Select Committee on Nationalised Industries, Session 1976–77: The Role of British Rail in Public Transport.* H.M.S.O.
7. Cmnd 6836.
8. *Transport Act 1947.* H.M.S.O.
9. *Transport Act 1953.* H.M.S.O.
10. *Transport Act 1956.* H.M.S.O.
11. *Transport Act 1962.*
12. *ibid.*, section 10(i).
13. *Transport Act 1968.* Sections 39, 40 and 56.
14. Cmnd 3437 (1967) *Nationalised Industries: A Review of Economic and Financial Objectives.* H.M.S.O.
15. *A Study of the U.K. Nationalised Industries. Their Role in the Economy and Control in the Future.* 31–32.
16. *Railways Act 1974.*
17. E.E.C. Council Regulation 1191/69.
18. *Railways Act 1974.* Section 3.
19. *Transport Act 1947.*

20. *A Study of the U.K. Nationalised Industries. Their Role in the Economy and Control in the Future.* 38.
21. Peyton, John (28 November 1973) Ministerial Statement. Hansard.
22. Mulley, Fred (24 June 1974) Ministerial Statement. Hansard.
23. Cmnd 3656.
24. *ibid.* para 9.
25. *Transport Policy: A Consultation Document.* **1,** para 1.9.
26. Malcor, R. (1970) *Problèmes posés par l'application pratique d'une tarification pour l'usage des infrastructures routières.* Brussels. E.E. Studies, Transport Series 2.
27. Gwilliam, K. M., Petriccione, S., Voight, F. and Zighera, J. A. (1973) *Criteria for Co-ordination of Investments in Transport Infrastructures.* Brussels: E.E. Studies, Transport Series 3.
28. *Transport Policy: A Consultation Document.* **1,** Chapter 4.
29. *Transport Policy: An Opportunity for Change.* 9.

Chapter 8
1. Cmnd 7131. 24.
2. *A study of the U.K. Nationalised Industries. Their Role in the Economy and Control in the Future.*
3. *Transport Policy: An Opportunity for Change.* 30–31.
4. Accounting Standards Committee (April 1979) *Current Cost Accounting.* Exposure Draft 24.
5. For further details see Harris, D. J. (July–August, 1979) 'Risk Analysis and Financial Planning'. *Management Accountant.*
6. Cmnd 7131. 23–25.

Chapter 9
1. Cmnd 6836. 65.
2. Cmnd 7131.
3. Cmnd 6836. 62.
4. *ibid.* 48.
5: *ibid.* 40.
6. *ibid.* 49.
7. *Transport Policy: An Opportunity for Change.* 34.
8. Cmnd 6836. 37.
9. *Transport Policy: A Consultation Document.* **1,** 51.
10. Cmnd 6836. 29.
11. *Transport Policy: A Consultation Document.* **1,** 52.
12. Cmnd 6836. 20.
13. Williams, D. G. (1975) *The Application of Section 203 of the*

Local Government Act 1972. M.Sc. Dissertation, University of Bath.
14. Cmnd. 6836. 22.
15. *Transport Policy: A Consultation Document.* **1,** 51.
16. Cmnd 6836. 40.
17. *ibid.* 41.
18. *ibid.* 41.
19. *ibid.* 41.
20. *ibid.* 41.
21. *ibid.* 46.
22. Price Commission (1978) *British Railways Board–Increases in Passenger Fares.* H.M.S.O. 37.
23. *Transport Policy: An Opportunity for Change.* 42.
24. *ibid.* 60.
25. *The Rail Problem.* 136–184.

Chapter 10
1. Cmnd 6836. 62.
2. Cmnd 7841 (1980) The Government's Expenditure Plans 1980–81 to 1983–4. 62.
3. *ibid.* 151.

Index

195